CW01090641

The Prisoner of War Diary of Captain Frank Edward Elgar

The Prisoner of War Diary of Captain Frank Edward Elgar

THE SHERWOOD FORESTERS
(Nottinghamshire & Derbyshire Regiment)

Frank Elgar

First published in the United Kingdom in 2025 by
The Choir Press

ISBN 978-1-78963-502-7

Contents

Figures

Foreword

by Colonel Michael G. Scott

In March 1943, Captain Frank Edward Elgar was captured and taken as a prisoner of war by German forces, in North Africa, while serving with his regiment, the Sherwood Foresters. Elgar's POW Diary charts his odyssey and experiences in several POW camps over twenty-four months, from the time of his capture in Tunisia until March 1945, by which stage he was in Germany. His experiences in the next, final two months as a POW, prior to liberation by the Allies in May, are documented in a letter that he later wrote to a friend.

This transcript of Elgar's original manuscript POW Diary, charting his experiences during the two years of his captivity, forms an important historical record. Written in compelling and frank detail, his record is not only of great interest to his immediate family, but also to the wider public, as it provides a valuable insight into the rigours and routine of life in enemy POW camps during the Second World War.

Elgar's POW Diary is recorded in two 'books'. These books were provided in blank format to Allied POWs by the YMCA, through the auspices of the Red Cross. Those incarcerated were encouraged to record within their books anything of interest, thus providing the POWs with a means of documenting their experiences. We are fortunate that Elgar chose to utilise his books to such good effect. Moreover, it is also fortuitous that his POW Diary survives for, as will be related, periodically Elgar had to hide it, to guard against his captors confiscating and destroying it.

Book 1 of Elgar's POW Diary chronicles the time from his capture in Tunisia by the Germans, in March 1943, until the Italian Armistice of 3 September 1943. During this period, he was incarcerated in POW camps, under Italian authority, in Tunis, Capua, and Modena. Following the Italian Armistice, Elgar was moved north by German forces, and Book 2 of his Diary chronicles his time in POW camps in Moosburg (near Munich), Fort Bismark (Strasbourg), and Weinsberg (near Stuttgart).

Elgar's German POW Card[1] records his prisoner number as 2536. He started writing his POW Diary in February 1944, eleven months after his capture, by which stage he was imprisoned in Weinsberg.[2] In March 1945, Elgar and fellow POWs at Weinsberg were transported by the Germans to Moosburg, as documented in a letter to a friend and fellow POW, an excerpt of which forms the sequel to this narrative. It was from Moosburg that he was liberated by Allied forces, in May 1945, and repatriated to England.

No endeavour is made within this foreword to provide a synopsis of Elgar's POW experiences, and so we shall allow his Diary alone to narrate that story. However, Elgar's military service commenced well before the fateful night in March 1943 when, while leading his troops on a reconnaissance patrol, he was captured in Tunisia. None of this earlier service is covered within his Diary, and therefore it is worth outlining here, by way of background, something of Elgar's earlier regimental service prior to his capture.

Elgar commenced officer training just a few weeks after the outbreak of the Second World War, which started on 1 September 1939 with Germany's invasion of Poland. On 3 September, Britain declared war on Germany. Having initially been enlisted with an Army Number of 6464009 into the Royal Fusiliers (City of London Regiment), Elgar reported to the Royal Military Academy, Sandhurst, to undertake a short, four-month war course. The *Sandhurst Cadet Register* records him as being aged twenty-two, having a college admission date of 27 October 1939, and a departure date of 24 February 1940, just a week following his twenty-third birthday.[3]

Elgar successfully 'passed out' of Sandhurst, having served the same amount of training time at the Academy as all other cadets in his intake. He was 'gazetted' on 1 March 1940 in the rank of second lieutenant, with effect from 25 February, with an officer's Army Number of 121204 and a commission in the Sherwood Foresters. Elgar was one of three subal-

---

[1]   The National Archives [TNA], War Office [WO] 416/110/180, German POW Card, Captain Frank E. Elgar.
[2]   See: TNA, WO 208/3289, Oct 1943-Dec 1945, for a general synopsis on OFLAG VA Weinsberg.
[3]   Sandhurst Cadet Entries, Royal Military Academy. Date of Birth 16 February 1917.

terns from his Sandhurst intake who joined the Sherwood Foresters, all of whom had originally been enlisted into the Royal Fusiliers.[4]

The Sherwood Foresters (Nottinghamshire and Derbyshire Regiment) was a line infantry regiment, founded in 1881. In due course the regiment merged, in 1970, with the Worcestershire Regiment to form the Worcestershire and Sherwood Foresters, which in turn merged, in 2007, with the Cheshire Regiment and the Staffordshire Regiment to form the present Mercian Regiment.

During the Second World War a dozen or so battalions of the Sherwood Foresters were raised. The 1st and 2nd Battalions were both pre-war Regular units. The other battalions were Territorial Army units, the majority of which were newly raised because of the war, many of which, similarly to their Regular counterparts, saw service overseas.

The 2nd Sherwood Foresters, with which Elgar primarily served, had sailed for France the previous year in September 1939 shortly after the outbreak of war. As part of the British Expeditionary Force (BEF), the battalion was engaged in the 'Phoney War', the eight-month period at the start of the war during which the French invasion of (and subsequent withdrawal from) Germany's Saar district had been the only military land operation on the Western Front.

Other battalions of the Sherwood Foresters also joined the BEF. These included the 1/5th, the 2/5th (later renamed the 5th) and 9th Battalions. Later, the 2nd, the 2/5th and 9th Battalions were all involved in defending the Dunkirk perimeter before the eventual evacuation, while the 1/5th Battalion was evacuated from Cherbourg.

Following Sandhurst training, Elgar was initially posted to 1/5th Sherwood Foresters, under the command of Lieutenant Colonel H.H. Lilly, and is recorded in the Battalion's War Diary nominal roll of 14 April 1940 as having joined the unit on 12 April, as one of seven second lieutenants, from No.1 Infantry Base Depot.[5] The depot provided Elgar and fellow officer reinforcements with additional, specific-to-theatre military training before they joined their units. Of these seven subalterns, two of them (Patrick Hughes and John Goatly) had been 'gazetted' to the Sherwood Foresters, following Sandhurst, at the same time as Elgar.

---

[4]   London Gazette (Supplement 34802, Page 1234), 1 March 1940.
[5]   TNA, WO 167/824, war diary 1/5th Sherwood Foresters, (BEF/France) Apr-May 1940; WO 167/823, war diary 2nd Sherwood Foresters, (BEF/France) Jan-Jun 1940.

However, having arrived with the 1/5th Battalion, Elgar is recorded as being posted very soon thereafter, on 27 April, to 2nd Sherwood Foresters, along with two others (Patrick Hughes and T.B. Tirbutt) from his draft of seven subalterns. A fourth subaltern from that draft of seven (T.C. Blagg) followed them to the 2nd Battalion soon afterwards, on 2 May.

Elgar's battalion, the 2nd Sherwood Foresters, served in 3rd Infantry Brigade, part of 1st Infantry Division, with which the battalion remained throughout the war. Besides 2nd Sherwood Foresters, the 3rd Infantry Brigade was comprised of the 1st Duke of Wellington's Regiment, the 1st King's Shropshire Light Infantry, and 3rd Infantry Brigade Anti-Tank Company. The 1st Infantry Division formed part of I Corps of the BEF, and 3rd Infantry Brigade served alongside the French Army on the Maginot Line, on the Franco-Belgian border during the Phoney War, until German forces invaded France and the low countries on 10 May 1940.

Reporting for duty with 2nd Sherwood Foresters, under the command of Lieutenant Colonel G.M. Gamble, at the end of April 1940, Elgar therefore joined his battalion at the very end of the Phoney War. For within just a fortnight Germany invaded France and the low countries. The Battle of France (also dubbed the Fall of France) began on 10 May, the day that Winston Churchill became Prime Minister. As vanguard to 3rd Infantry Brigade, 2nd Sherwood Foresters crossed the border from France into Belgium and reached Brussels on 11 May. However, within just a few days the enemy forced the Brigade to withdraw.

By 14 May, German forces had successfully launched a surprise advance through the Ardennes and the Somme valley. Their armoured forces then manoeuvred to cut off and surround those Allied forces which had advanced into Belgium ready to meet the anticipated German invasion. Despite Allied counterattacks, German forces reached the coast by 20 May, and then turned north up towards the English Channel. In doing so they trapped and separated those Allied forces, including the BEF, from most of the French troops further to the south.

Then, on 24 May, the Germans halted their advance on Dunkirk for three days, in order to consolidate and avoid any possible Allied breakout. This contentious decision, later known as the 'Halt Order', which was not rescinded until 26 May, had the effect of stalling German momentum. Moreover, it provided the BEF with three precious days to build a defensive line, fight back to the west, and organise the evacuation of Dunkirk. German forces then re-launched their drive to push British, French and Belgian forces back to the sea.

By this stage, 26 May, with the Allies losing the Battle of France and the BEF and French 1st Army surrounded by German forces, the BEF's 1st Infantry Division, amongst others, was under heavy attack. The Allies were contained within a corridor to the sea, some sixty miles deep and fifteen miles wide, with most of the BEF centred upon Lille, some forty miles from Dunkirk. That same day, while the BEF's 2nd Division kept the corridor open, the BEF's 1st Infantry Division, along with its 3rd, 4th, and 42nd Divisions, retreated west along the corridor to the coast, taking heavy casualties in the process. As they withdrew the Allies destroyed their artillery, vehicles, and stores, to deny them to the enemy.

Thus, Elgar took part in the short and bitter fighting in the latter part of May, with 2nd Sherwood Foresters, in which the BEF's 1st Infantry Division was engaged. During which time, the British were forced back to the sea by German forces.[6]

That same day marked the start of the Battle of Dunkirk, from 26 May to 4 June, the defence and evacuation to England by sea of the BEF and other Allied forces. By the following day, 27 May, the BEF had fought back to the Dunkirk perimeter line. This defensive line, semi-circular in nature, was defended by French forces in the western sector and by the British in the east. A confused battle raged all along the perimeter on 28 May, the day that Belgian forces surrendered, and the Germans inexorably drove the perimeter inwards towards Dunkirk. Nonetheless, Allied forces were able to hold the Dunkirk perimeter throughout 29-30 May and, despite breaches made in the line by the Germans on 31 May, in desperate fighting the Allies grimly held their defensive line.

During the Dunkirk evacuation, Operation Dynamo, that took place in the nine days between 27 May and 4 June, some 338,000 men were evacuated. These included the BEF, and French, Polish, Belgian and some Dutch troops.

The 2nd Sherwood Foresters, as part of 3rd Infantry Brigade, were evacuated from Dunkirk by SS *Malines* to England on 31 May. However, just a few days previously, on 28 May, the Battalion's commanding officer, Lieutenant Colonel G.M. Gamble, had been wounded and the Adjutant, Captain W.P. Allsebrook, killed by a shell. The Battalion therefore disembarked at Folkestone, Kent and proceeded to Tidworth, Hampshire

---

6   See: Masters, John W.A., *The Story of The 2nd Battalion The Sherwood Foresters 1939-1945* (Gale & Polden, 1946).

to reform, under the command of Major (later Lieutenant Colonel) J.E. Wright, who had hitherto been the Battalion's second-in-command.[7]

The last of the BEF were evacuated by 3 June, followed by many of the French rear-guard troops in the early hours of the following morning. German forces captured Dunkirk before noon on 4 June, taking prisoner over half of the French rear-guard troops in the process. Soon thereafter, on 14 June, the Germans occupied Paris unopposed, and an armistice was signed on 22 June. Thus, in just six weeks, from 10 May 1940, during the Battle of France, German forces conquered France, Belgium, the Netherlands, and Luxembourg. This ended land operations on the Western Front for some four years, until the Allied Normandy invasion on 6 June 1944.

Following the BEF's retreat from Dunkirk, 2nd Sherwood Foresters remained in the United Kingdom on Home Defence duties. There it prepared for a German invasion which never came, until early in 1943 when the battalion was sent to North Africa to take part in the Campaign in Tunisia.

Throughout the latter half of 1940, in UK with Home Forces, it is evident that 2nd Sherwood Foresters, by then based in Spilsby, Lincolnshire, was recovering from Dunkirk. However, by the end of that year the Battalion had started to field sports teams against other Army units, and Elgar is thereafter routinely listed as being in the Battalion's rugby team. Moreover, he is also listed as attending various military courses of instruction, and often being in receipt of 'field allowance', for the Battalion was spending a good deal of time on 'field manoeuvre' military training. Elgar was promoted from second lieutenant to lieutenant in August 1941, and by early 1942 he was promoted to temporary captain.[8]

Allied fortunes turned in the North African Campaign, following the British Eighth Army's victory in the 2nd Battle of El Alamein in October 1942, a battle in which the 14th Sherwood Foresters took part. This represented a major turning point in the war, and by 4 November Rommel's *Panzerarmee Afrika* was in retreat, with the Eighth Army hot on its heels.

---

[7]   See: Barclay, C.N., *The History of The Sherwood Foresters (Nottinghamshire and Derbyshire Regiment) 1919-1957*, (William Clowes, 1959).

[8]   TNA, WO 166/4663, war diary 2nd Sherwood Foresters, (Home Forces) Jul-Dec 1940; WO 166/4664, war diary 2nd Sherwood Foresters, (Home Forces) 1941; 166/8954, war diary 2nd Sherwood Foresters, (Home Forces) 1942; WO 166/12704, war diary 2nd Sherwood Foresters, (Home Forces) Jan 1943.

The previous year America had entered the war, following the Japanese attack on Pearl Harbour, and joint Anglo-US forces were now poised to land in French North-West Africa.

On 8 November, during Operation Torch, these Anglo-US forces landed in Algeria and Morocco. The plan was that once the French Vichy territories of Morocco, Algeria and Tunisia had been secured, these same Allied forces would thrust east against Axis forces in the Western Desert, while the Eighth Army continued to pursue Rommel westwards. Once the whole of the North African coastline was in Allied hands, this would then allow the Mediterranean to be opened to Allied shipping.

However, Anglo-US forces met extremely stiff resistance from Axis forces in the Tunisian Campaign, and it took the Allies six months before they eventually trapped Axis forces in Tunis, where they eventually surrendered in May 1943. In the interim, following the Torch landings in the first three months of 1943, the British First Army, comprising the 6th Armoured and 78th Infantry Divisions, received a further three British divisions as reinforcements, including the 1st, the 4th, and 46th Infantry Divisions.

The 1st Infantry Division sailed from England for North Africa in late February 1943, arriving there in early March. With 1st Infantry Division came its 3rd Infantry Brigade, of which 2nd Sherwood Foresters, now under the command of Lieutenant Colonel R.T.K. Pye, was still a component unit. By this stage the 2/5th Battalion (by now renamed the 5th Sherwood Foresters) was already in theatre, having arrived in January with one of the other reinforcement divisions. Initially placed directly under command of the British First Army, the 1st Infantry Division was subsequently placed under command of the British V Corps, as First Army expanded in size with its reinforcement divisions to the strength of two corps.

The War Diary of 2nd Sherwood Foresters confirms that Elgar embarked with the Battalion, as Second-in-Command of 'A' Company, at Avonmouth, Bristol on 25 February 1943, and that the unit disembarked on 9 March at Algiers. The 1st Infantry Division was allocated the Medjez-Bou Arada Sector, south-west of Tunis, and began preparing for the coming offensive. April saw the Division engaged in particularly hard fighting against German forces, at Sedjenane and at the Battle of Medjez Plain. However, in the interim a vital part of the Division's preparations was patrolling activity to assess the positions and strength of the Hermann Goering Division, the German formation against which they were pitted.

Thus, it was that on the night of 23/24 March 1943, while leading six soldiers on a reconnaissance patrol, just north of Bou Arada, Elgar came to be taken POW by soldiers of the Hermann Goering Division. Regarding that fateful night when he was captured, the following is recorded in the Battalion War Diary: '*A Coy [Company] contact with enemy. Pte [Private] Bowler returns alone. Capt [Captain] F.E. Elgar and 5 ORs [other ranks] missing."* "*B Coy Patrol - Pte Henton killed, one Pte missing, believed killed.* "*C Coy Patrol - Cpl [Corporal] Neave missing, believed killed*'.[9] It is at this stage that the story is taken up by Elgar in his POW Diary.

Shortly after Elgar's capture, the Allies prevailed in North Africa, having first trapped the Axis forces in Tunis, where they surrendered on 13 May 1943. Following the successful North African campaign, the 2nd Sherwood Foresters, still part of 3rd Infantry Brigade, of 1st Infantry Division were dispatched in June to capture the Italian island of Pantelleria, which they accomplished without casualties. At the end of that year the Division then joined the British Eighth Army, fighting in Italy. In January 1944, the Division next took part in the Anzio assault landings and, over the next twelve months, fought their way up the length of Italy. At the end of January 1945, the 3rd Infantry Brigade was sent to garrison Palestine, which is where 2nd Sherwood Foresters then remained until the end of the war at the beginning of September 1945.

Meanwhile, in early April 1945, Elgar and his fellow POWs in Oflag V-A at Weinsberg were moved, by train, back to Stalag VII-A at Moosburg, near Munich. At the end of April, American troops of the US 3rd Army, under General George S. Patton, captured Munich. Nearby, 35 miles away, Stalag VII-A was liberated by troops of the US 14th Armoured Division on 29 April, and Patton visited the POW camp and its inmates there at Moosburg a few days later.[10]

Elgar and his fellow POWs were flown to Brussels the next week, where on 8 May (V-E Day) they heard of the German surrender. The following day Elgar was repatriated to England, via Abbeville, landing on home soil at Wing Airfield, Buckinghamshire. A fellow Sherwood Forester and POW, Richard Garrett (5th Sherwood Foresters), with

---

[9]   TNA, WO 175/521, war diary 2nd Sherwood Foresters, (North Africa) Feb-Jun 1943.
[10]   Reither, Dr. Dominik., *The End of the War in Moosburg*, (*Moosburger Zeitung*, April 2020).

whom Elgar had shared a room at Weinsberg, later wrote a book on his wartime experiences,[11] while their return to England was featured in the documentary, *The Day the War Ended*, on BBC television.

Upon repatriation to England, and with his father by this stage seriously ill, Elgar was demobilised.[12] Some four months later, on 15 August 1945, V-J Day was declared and a fortnight later, following Japan's formal surrender aboard the battleship USS *Missouri* in Tokyo Bay, the end of the war was proclaimed. By this stage, Elgar was looking to the future and attending night classes to qualify as a chartered surveyor, so that he could take charge of the family firm of land agents in Kent.

---

[11] Garrett R., *Great Escapes of World War II, And Some That Failed to Make It*, (Weidenfeld & Nicolson, London, 1989).

[12] Army Service Record: the exact date of Frank E. Elgar's demobilisation is unclear, as although the Elgar family applied for a copy of his Army Service Record, the Army Personnel Centre, Glasgow, responded, in 2022, that it could not be found.

Glossary, Abbreviations and Acronyms

4.2" Mortar	Ordnance ML 4.2-inch Mortar [used by British infantry]
ack ack	anti-aircraft guns
Arty	artillery
BD	Battle Dress
BEF	British Expeditionary Force
Bn	Battalion
Bosch	German enemy
Bully	Bully Beef (Corned Beef)
Cheshires	Cheshire Regiment
civvy	civilian
CNA	Central News Agency
Coldstreams	Coldstream Guards
Coy	Company
Coy Cmdr	Company Commander
CSM	Company Sergeant Major
DLI	Durham Light Infantry
FO	Flying Officer [rank, in air force]
Grenadiers / GG	Grenadier Guards
Hermann Goerings	Hermann Goering Division
HQ(s) / Hqr(s)	Headquarter(s)
Innickillings [sic]	Royal Inniskilling Fusiliers
IO	Intelligence Officer
It(i)e(s)	Italian(s)

Jerry / Jerries	German enemy
JU 52	Junkers JU 52 [German transport aircraft]
kuss kuss	Couscous [made with semolina / durum wheat flour]
Lincolns	Lincolnshire Regiment
ME	Messerschmitt ME 109 [German fighter aircraft]
MG	machine gun
Midlothian	Midlothian Artillery Volunteers
MO	Medical Officer
Monty	General Bernard Montgomery, Commander Eighth Army
morphia	morphine [old-fashioned terminology]
NA	North Africa
NCO(s)	Non Commissioned Officer(s)
Oflag	Offizierslager [German POW camp for officers]
OFW	Oberfeldwebel [rank, equivalent to a Warrant Officer Class 2]
OP	observation post
OR(s)	Other Rank(s)
Pln(s)	platoon(s)
pom-poms	Royal Navy 2-pounder, anti-aircraft, 40mm canon
posn(s)	position(s)
POW	Prisoner of War
PT	physical training
Pte(s)	Private(s) [rank, lowest in British Army]
QM	Quartermaster
RA	Royal Artillery
RAAF	Royal Australian Air Force
recce	reconnaissance
Rly	railway
RSM	Regimental Sergeant Major
SBO	Senior British Officer

Schmeisser	MP40 submachine gun [German, 9mm calibre]
Sgt	sergeant
sub(s)	submarine(s)
Very / Verey	flare light
Wog(s)	'Arab' native [North Africa, in this instance]
Wop(s)	Italian enemy
YMCA	Young Men's Christian Association

Preface to Third Volume: Moosburg near Munich

Perhaps it is vanity, perhaps it is a desire that the lessons of experience shall not be forgotten, probably it is a combination of the two; but most of us wish to retain some evidence of our impressions as P.O.Ws, though others profess that they desire to forget this phase of their lives as swiftly as possible. The majority however are using these 'logs' for drawings, photographs, sketches, paintings and 'scraps' which they insert with such assiduousness that it is obvious they wish to retain a vivid memory of their experiences as prisoners.

I feel sure that this desire to perpetuate one's impressions, is not solely for the purpose of 'showing off' when one returns home; it is so strong that I am convinced that it is due to a feeling, however vague and uncertain, that some valuable lessons have been learnt which it would be unwise to forget. And such is our state of mind that forgetfulness is only too likely.

It would be easy, but quite useless to enumerate the various lessons one has learnt, but such a list would indeed be a mere "lesson" and a dead one at that. In order to learn something properly, you have to experience it; you can by means of a book discover how to swim but until you have actually plunged into the water and swum, you cannot be said to have learnt how to swim. That is why exams are so trying.

Therefore in order to re-learn our lessons, we must re-live our experiences; we dare not trust to memory alone, hence the painstaking care with which these books are filled in. This book is an exception, of course; I had hoped to fill it with pictures – sketches, paintings, drawings etc. but alas I am no artist, and those who are have more important things to do. Thus there is only one thing to do, I must use words to describe what would be much better expressed in a picture:

It is Sunday evening, 25 March 1945; once more hopes are high, the allies have crossed the Rhine.

The news came yesterday, so that we are still uncertain as to what is happening and many fear that we may be moved, perhaps violently.

Today the drone and whine of cruising and diving planes has been almost incessant. For eleven and a quarter hours the 'alert' or 'alarm' has been 'on'.

Now I am sitting in our room (25/5). My pullover for a cushion, three bulbs of 20 watts each supply inadequate light, my battle dress blouse is a little tight and I have just laid down "Selected Essays" of Hilaire Belloc, although I was in the middle of a criticism of Rasselus.

I am sitting at the smaller of our two tables, Ted and Arthur Duvine are talking about the police and are seated on my left; Richard Garrett[1] who was on my right, reading, has now gone out of the room. On the other table, a game of bridge is in progress. Michael Davies is playing the hand, Brian Lasc as dummy is talking – food question if we are moved – Jack Henning and Lane, the latter complaining about his cards – make up the four. Taffy and David Jones Williams are talking about the war … "two to one" ... "Yes … Necller Valley … Klim yet … yes … bash … three hundred ..." occasional words reach me. Bob Nixon, who rigged up the light with two bulbs where only one was intended, is working at the far end of the large table beyond the bridge players. Opposite me Ray Lever lies on his bed feeling slightly bilious.

It is warm, many of us are in shorts. Some towels, handkerchiefs and odd pieces of clothing hang on string, tied across the room in seeming disorder, but in fact so arranged that their burdens shall not obscure the light. The shaving water is in a large black tin on the fire, a red Canadian Butter tin is beside it. The door is open behind me and Jack Todd has just wandered in.

---

[1]   A prolific author of several books about WWII and POW's.

Book 1: Tunis, Capua, Modena

INTRODUCTION BOOK 1

It is now 26 of Feb. 1944 [diary date], and I intend to write a diary of the events that have occurred since the day of my capture in North Africa in March 1943. Owing to the lapse of time such a diary cannot be very full or very accurate and I am very dubious as to the result. However if it is successful, I shall be in a strong position on my return home to meet the inevitable barrage of questions from friends and relatives. "You want to know what happened? You wish to know the why and the wherefore – Very well my friends, everything of importance is in this little blue book, read it for yourselves and be satisfied." A very unfair method of defence; a most escapist attitude to adopt, but for all that the diary is to be written. Whether any of my friends will be (a) sufficiently foolish to want to read it and (b) sufficiently agile of eye to be able to read it, is really, beside the point. The threat will be there "Question me about my life as a P.O.W. and I shall give you my diary to read through; I very much doubt if you will be able to do so."

23 MARCH 1943

The Bn [Battalion] is just north of Bou Arada and my company is defending "Grand stand". We have been here about a week and have done much work on the defences; mining, wiring, digging alternative positions etc. My Coy Cmdr. [Company Commander] Aubrey Phillips has shown his usual shrewdness and a grasp of the essentials. When I took over from the Innickillings [sic; i.e. 6th Battalion, Royal Inniskilling Fusiliers, of 38th (Irish) Infantry Brigade] I was very depressed by the muddle and lack of coordination in the defence plan. They had had too many casualties to do much work on the place themselves. However things are straightened out now. Opposite us are the Hermann Goerings [i.e. The Hermann Goering Division] who are, according to intelligence, a fairly tough crowd, they have come from Russia so they are veterans but have been made up to strength from very young and inexperienced soldiers. A few mortar bombs and infantry gun shells have arrived daily usually at midday and about 1700 hrs. At stand-to each morning they let fly with an M.G. [machine gun] from Gravel Pit Hill, the 3" mortars have registered this hill now, so we can now reply. Today we have been digging a Coy [Company] Battle H.Q. it looks pretty good, but is difficult to conceal. Hope the Heavenly Twins (Two [Messerschmitt] M.Es that fly over daily on Recce) will not spot it.

Bayer was to have gone out on patrol tonight; now I have got the job. Six of us to recce [reconnaissance patrol] behind Plough Top hill. Just before dark got an intelligence report on the locality of one German Company and two Plns. [platoons] Two of these Posns. [positions] are very close to the route I have chosen. Laid on Arty [Artillery] Fire on Wog Hill where we suspect there is an M.G. position.

–

The patrol started badly, we had difficulty locating the gap in our minefield though I had asked B– to act as a guide for this. We went on a compass bearing, then I slipped and fell and I think put the instrument out of adjustment; soon we saw we were heading for Wog Hill and remembered our own artillery would shell it if they heard or saw signs of a scrap. Then we heard a German patrol and I think they suspected us, anyway up went a Verey light, to get round them we had to go still further left and still further off our route. [It was] very dark, misty, moon not up yet; the ideal night. We moved around our right crawling and walking, stopping and listening. Then a guard dog started barking; that was not unusual, they bark every night, but it was soon obvious that he was barking at us and following us; could not see to shoot him but he saw us stalking him and ran off. But the damage was done; a German M.G. opened up. Thanks to the tracer I could spot where it was and made a mental note of it; I might have thanked that dog for inducing the Bosch [German enemy] to open up and give his position away had he not also warned them of our approach. We still had not reached our objective, we had been going for over two hours and the moon was rising, and although it was past midnight it seemed horribly light. At last we could see our objective and then one of my men was sick, why I don't know, overtired I expect; said that he could carry on. The ground was horribly open; we clung to what shadow and cover there was; the moon was up and except for an occasional cloud, shone with disconcerting brilliance. Then we found a dead German, he had been seen by a patrol on the previous night and I knew that we had not much further to go. At last the shell-battered remains of a few Wog Huts [Arab (native) huts] which we had to search, could be seen. They were empty. But for a British steel helmet and pack; no booby traps; came across barbed wire 1" above ground, but no mines beyond it; no machine guns either, in fact no sign of life. The hills nearby seemed devoid of life but we had to make sure. They were. No sign of Bosch except that wire. At last I was satisfied and we set off for our own lines. The moon was still very bright, and we had not gone more than a few hundred yards when we were challenged by a German sentry; he was some way off and fired a V. light [Verey light] into the air; we could [hear] several of them but apparently they did not spot us; we crawled on, worming our way through the sparse vegetation. Then machine guns opened up, there were shouts in German and lights were again fired, the tracers whipped over our heads and we ran by bounds covering each other from bound to bound. We seemed to be quite clear, but I was not sure of our position. The numerous hills looked weirdly alike and were difficult to recognise. But we set off again in the direction of our own lines. Again we were challenged this time in front of us from a wadi. We began to worm our way forward hoping to spot and deal with the sentry. Soon we could see him and I was about to fire when the sergeant beside me whispered look out Sir there are dozens of 'em on our right. And then the inevitable Verey light was fired and two machine guns let fly; this time they were very close and to attempt to shoot our way through with three Tommy guns, a revolver and a rifle seemed hopeless. So we split up into pairs and tried to creep through unobserved. Grenades were thrown at the Sgt [Sergeant] and myself but no damage was done. Twelve of them then started to search for us shouting "Unds Up", they missed us and again we crept forward and I hoped we were through. But they started to search again, lobbing grenades and shouting "Unds Up" as before. Again it looked as though they had missed us, but apparently we had been seen for another party came up behind us and we found ourselves looking down the wrong end of a Schmeisser. [MP40 submachine gun] I was bitterly disappointed we had been taken without firing a round. And I wish we had risked a scrap to get through; evidently the German officer saw this, for he said "For you the War is over Yes?" I made no reply. "You would never have got through I assure you", he went on, "we have a strong position here". He was right, there was a company in that river bed and in the open, as we were, we stood no chance. But I still felt furious and could only hope the other 3 might get through. "How many were there of you", asked the German. "Guess", I replied. "I know there are five at least", he said. Two more of my men then appeared, one of them badly wounded in the hand. The Bosch treated him well, bound his hand up and got him back to hospital; giving him morphia to relieve the pain. One man was still missing – Pte [Private] Bowler – and I hoped he had got away but to this day I do not know if in fact he did. The Germans kept asking us about him, but we never said a word.

It was now about 3 o'clock in the morning. And though we were in no man's land, the Bosch, as soon as they had searched us, gave us cigarettes and displayed great jubilation in that they had captured an Officer. I suppose I should have been flattered. Then we walked back up the dry river bed escorted by a German Sgt and two Ptes. We passed several Booby Traps – cunningly concealed trip wires etc. and went back to a German O.P. [observation post] where the Germans obviously had a telephone. We were left to ourselves for a bit though closely watched, and I told the others that we were bound to be questioned and that they were to say nothing. I also apologised to them for the mess we were in; I could not thank them enough for that cheery way they took it, assuring me that we were just unlucky and so on. It seems rather fatuous writing this now, but it meant a lot at the time to know that one's men bore no ill will. I thought of Aubrey waiting in our O.P. wondering what had become of us. He had lost three Tommy guns and five very good men; never have I felt so depressed. However, self-pity is of no avail, our duty was obvious; escape if possible and say nothing when questioned.

We were taken back further into the German lines; and I noticed that no barbed wire was used; the Coy H.Q. was a concrete dug out as were the men's rest quarters. There was a small weapon pits, beautifully concealed in cactus bushes etc. There were many positions which were not manned, and all seemed to be sited for concealment rather than for fields of fire. All round protection was poor, but in the hills they had made full use of defilade. The same German officer tried to draw me into conversation; he spoke English well and told me that he had been in England for several years and knew Leeds well.

It was now first light and we were escorted back to Battalion Hqrs. [Headquarters] As we moved along, our artillery started firing. One of my guards – little more than a boy – said "Ach, Wump, Wump, Wump", and made a face at me. I felt better then.

We reached Battalion Headquarters and were again searched. By now we were tired, very hungry and cold. We waited for several hours, the Colonel asked me what I thought of Churchill; without waiting for a reply he said "I wonder you trust him." What a chance: "Do you trust Hitler[?]" I asked, "Remember Stalingrad, what did you as an experienced soldier think of that effort." He merely muttered "Ach", and walked off. Life looked a little brighter. Meanwhile my men were also doing a little propaganda on their own with a German Corporal who spoke good English. He started by asking "When will the war end?" "When we have won", my sergeant replied, "perhaps by next Christmas." "We shall soon drive you out of Africa", said the German – "Oh Yeah, you said that before El Alamein and now look where you are." And so the argument went on. It was quite clear that the Germans had lost a lot of confidence; and as far as our captors were concerned we did all we could to make them lose a bit more.

We were taken by truck back to what I suppose was Brigade Headquarters, the journey was in a Mercedes truck and the first part of the going was along a very bumpy and muddy track; as this track was in range and sight of our artillery, we went as fast as possible; lurching, sliding and bumping in a sea of mud. No shells arrived. I noticed as we were leaving, a German officer talking to some filthy looking Arabs; they were given money I think, and set off in the direction of our lines. The German corporal looked at me. "We know how to treat the Arabs", he said. "We show them a gun. 'This for any disobedience' and then we show them money – 'This for you if you serve us well'."

When we reached Brigade Headquarters two of my men were questioned and one was threatened that if he did not speak he would be shot. They both seemed very pleased with themselves and assured me they had not answered a single question. Except their name, rank and number. From the latter they knew our regiment but did not know which Bn, which of course is what they really wanted. It was now about midday and we were all very hungry but were given no food; it was a glorious day the sun shone on the white dusty roads; Arabs could be seen working on their farms, driving carts and carrying on their normal peaceful everyday life. Now and again a distant rumble reminded one of the war, but apart from these rounds even the Germans looked peaceful.

Once more we were driven off in the truck, heading towards Tunis. There seemed to be very little German traffic on the roads, and apart from a petrol dump and occasional transport park concealed in cactus and poplar groves, there were few Germans to be seen; but there were Arabs everywhere, all dressed like scarecrows, a few French peasants in blue trousers were to be seen and as the road wound its way through hills and valleys, it seemed a good place for an escape. But we were wedged in between our guards, so could only wait and hope. We stopped by a deserted road junction, with no houses or other sign of human life.

"They are going to put us up against the wall", whispered the Sgt grinning. But we had stopped for the usual natural reason and soon pushed on again. The German Corporal, obviously quite a veteran, told me he had been in France and at Stalingrad. "War here", he said "is that of gentlemen. Russia was hell." I egged him on and he told me all his experiences. He had been to Singapore in peace time, "However did you lose such a fine base as that?" He loathed the Italians, but he said he respected the British, "Your artillery is terrible, but we could make even better use of it if we had it." "You are short of artillery here", I enquired innocently. He looked a little uneasy, then became confidential. "Why are we fighting, you and I, we are of the same blood, we should be fighting together not against each other." This argument was to become very familiar in the future but I was a rather surprised at the time. (Addenda. The Corporal tried hard to impress me with the excellence of the German POW camp.)

About 5 miles outside Tunis we stopped at the Div. H.Q. of the first Hermann Goerings. Here I was questioned by the Intelligence Officer, he spoke English with a slight accent and rather oddly. He tried the old dodge of a 'friendly chat', you know; I know you are ordered to answer no questions so we will talk of things other than the war. We had been warned about this, but it was so blatantly obvious that I laughed. After much talking on his part I was sent away and then my men were again questioned. They came out followed by a very irritated looking Intelligence Officer; good lads they had told him nothing except where he got off. The examination was conducted in a large room, before two new and very tough guards, the inevitable Arab was kept in the background.

We stayed at this HQ for the rest of the day; it was a French farm house; the farmer was still there and I tried to talk to him but my guards had other ideas. By six o'clock that night we were all very tired and extremely hungry (at least so we thought at the time, but we were to learn what hunger meant later). We were unshaven, unwashed, our faces were still black from the cork we had put on before setting out on our patrol. We had ordinary shoes or gym shoes on our feet instead of boots, and had found them unsuitable for walking the distances that we had done.

Eventually we managed to get a wash and I asked for some food. –"Later you shall eat", was the reply.

After dark I was told that the General wished me to drink some wine with him; the I.O. [Intelligence Officer] led me to the Officers mess tent; I went in and saluted the General. He was tall, dark, clean shaven, good looking with an intelligent face. He looked about 45 or 50 and was unable to speak a word of English. We carried on a laboured conversation through the I.O. who acted as an interpreter. I was introduced to the M.O. [Medical Officer] who had operated on the Pte who was wounded. He had had to amputate his hand and assured me that the man would be well looked after. But I should not be able to see him as he was in hospital. The I.O. then said "The General wishes to chat with you and appreciates that as a soldier you will tell us nothing of military importance." I replied in some way or other and was invited to sit down, and have a drink and some cakes. "How about my men?" I said "I can not eat and drink if they do not." I was assured that they would be fed so sat down and drank some wine – Chianti I think – the cakes were rather like dough nuts but a lighter brown in colour; afterwards I discovered that the Arabs made them; I often wonder under what kind of sanitary conditions they were made.

General Schmidt told me he would like to offer me whiskey, they had obtained large supplies at Dunkirk but had now finished them. I wondered if they got our supplies, which were dumped a few miles outside that town, but did not say as much to the General. He paid me one or two heavy compliments about the way we had refused to give information when questioned. "Did you expect us to do so", I said. "No you British are very stolid," was the reply via the I.O. After saying that Britain and Germany should get together after the war he bid me good night, with one or two more heavy compliments. In all sincerity I thanked him for the meal (such as it was) and the M.O. for looking after Pte –. I rejoined my men who were tucking into brown bread and some very dry cheese. We spent the night locked in a loose box; it was clean and had plenty of straw and we slept like logs.

25 MARCH 1943

Awoke feeling much better for our sleep. We were given a large dish of hot stew mostly rice, meat and spaghetti. My word it was good. At about 10 a.m. we set off for Tunis, and arrived there after about an hour.

First we stopped at a private house occupied by Germans; here we were photographed, our shoes attracted much attention. Next we were taken to the German prison camp. This was a school which had been taken over and was well and truly wired up. The occupants were all unshaven, mostly unwashed, all hungry, depressed and very near despair. They were mostly Americans, a few Free French, some Moroccan troops, several blacks and one and all had beards and looked desperately fed up.

I was again questioned this time by a fat, greasy German, an arrant Nazi to whom I took an instant dislike. We were both rude to each other and I told him nothing beyond the obvious fact that the German fighting troops with less amenities had treated us far better than those at the base. This obviously annoyed him. And then he produced photographs of the 4.2" Mortar [Ordnance ML 4.2-inch Mortar] in position obviously taken by an Arab behind our lines. I told him nothing about this weapon, and added that if he wanted to know more about it you should try the German front line. Finally, he fixed me with a sly and knowing grin "and how are the second fifth Foresters". I nearly jumped, the silly ass had got the wrong Bn. The 2/5 has been in N.A. [North Africa] longer than we had and were in a different division. Thus the Germans could not know that our division was now in the line. Then I was allowed to go and wandered out into the compound.

"Dinner up," bellowed a black-bearded American beating a large urn with a spoon. British to be served first. We queued up, we had no knives, forks, spoons, or plates. So washed out a steel helmet and used that; the food was what the Arabs call "kuss kuss" [i.e. Couscous] and consisted of a stew of some stuff rather like rice, mixed with grass or some vegetable exactly like grass; it looked, smelt and tasted – foul. Most of the prisoners were from the Eighth Army, and we learnt that the attack on the Mareth Line was due to start very soon. The great hope was that "Monty" [General Bernard Montgomery, Commander Eighth Army] would arrive before we left.

All British troops were then paraded and marched out of the camp; I as the only officer was allowed to march beside the men but not in the ranks. Most of the men were guardsmen from the 8th Army, a few D.L.Is [Durham Light Infantry] one or two Parachutists and various others.

One of the escort told me that we were being handed over to the Italians. The Germans kept all American prisoners and the Wops [Italian enemy] – all the British troops.

Tunis would be a delightful city if only it were cleaner; during our march to the Italian prison camp, we passed many Arabs, French and Italian civilians. And many German and Italian troops. Several people (the French particularly) gave us the V sign as covertly as possible. The Italians swore at us, the Arabs laughed and the German soldiers merely stared.

Eventually we arrived at the Italian P.O.W. Camp. This was situated in a shoe and rubber factory and contained about seven officers and 300

O.Rs. [other ranks] mostly 8th Army. As we arrived one officer appeared. "What's it like?" I asked. "Oh pretty bloody", was the reply.

Once inside we were given a printed blue card to send to our next-of-kin. We were disgusted when we read it – my dear – I am a prisoner of the Italians and am very well treated ... etc. "Two bloody lies to start with", said one Guardsman. We were given a Vatican telegram, on which we could write 25 words to our homes. That was on 25 March 43. I wonder when they got home.

Having filled in these forms, we joined the rest and faced a barrage of questions. How is Monty doing? When is the First Army going to wake up? Where were you captured? Who by? When? What is the latest news? and so on and so forth.

The factory consisted of two huge shops, one looking out on to the street, the other behind it; the two were under the same roof and were connected by a hanging door which could be raised or lowered from the front. The Officers were in a small room off the rear shop. All of us slept on concrete floors with the minimum of straw and the maximum of dust and discomfort. There were about 100 blankets between 300 or more; and many more prisoners arrived later but no more blankets. Such was our new abode. Perhaps I should add that in another annex was a large machine still oily and fairly clean but of this more anon.

One of the officers – Padre Gainess was already known to me, I met him at Woodhall Spa in Lincolnshire in 1942. He knew Robert Stott well as he had been Padre to his Bn. Derbyshire Yeo R.A. 8. Army.

The others were as follows in the list of officers on the next page. Many of the officers arrived after I did.

When I arrived, we had some sort of sing-song the same evening and I was requested to give them the latest news; the whole question was would Monty reach Tunis before we left.

We left Tunis on the 4th or 5th April so that I had about 10 days there; several of the officers were there for double that time. Compared to many P.O.Ws we were not so badly off, but for all that we had a very trying time. I was hungrier than I had ever been, even at Dunkirk. The Italians gave us hot coffee at breakfast (but no food); it was black and thin but sweet and warm. At midday we got about 1 ounce of meat or fish. A small loaf of bread every 3 days and 3 cigarettes per day. That was all. But the long arms of the Red Cross saved us literally from starvation. Every evening at 1700 hrs two women arrived accompanied by Italian soldiers staggering under the weight of two huge coppers of hot macaroni or spaghetti stew. Without any exaggeration this meal kept us alive. In addition,

Officers

R.C.K. Edwards	Recce Corps.	1st Army
Brian Lasc	D.L.I	1 "
'Scotty' White	"	8 "
Ian English	"	8 "
Bob Atherton	"	8 "
Wiggin	Grenadiers	8 "
Bonham Carter	"	8 "
Stamp. Brooksbanks	Coldstreams	8 "
Colin Leslie	first G	
Macdonald Smith	Derby. Yeo 1	
Sparkes	R.A.	
Bettel	R.A.	
Major Smith	R.A.	
Frank Whitehead	R.A.	
'Arny' Vivian	G.G.	8th
Sid "Burdett"	46 Recce.	
Tom Cocaine =	R.A.	1
Robire =		

these two French women took cash from us and purchased soap, tooth paste, razor blades etc. for us. These articles were very short in Tunis and they must have taken endless trouble to obtain what they did. In abominable French we tried to express our thanks.

We were well guarded, the Wop is so nervous that anything unusual upsets him and if we went anywhere near the barbed wire by night they shot at us. Many of the men had dysentery and as the latrines were revoltingly insanitary, being a mere trench already nearly full, swarming with flies, this disease increased tremendously.

After badgering the Italians, we at last obtained the necessary picks and shovels and dug a fresh latrine but left before it was properly completed. Led by the Padre we also tried to clear up the back yard which was the one open air place that we had. It was one mass of rubber shavings, tubes, tyres etc. rotting, stinking and filthy; we did our best and soon had a huge fire burning. The Italians became wildly excited and ordered us to put the fire out; we pretended we could not understand them and carried on with the good work, but eventually had to comply with their frantic orders – since we were at the more embarrassing end of the sentries' rifles.

The men were on the whole very good considering what they went through, but there were several rogues amongst them, who goaded on by hunger caused endless trouble. Our cigarette ration would not be quite sufficient, the food would not go all round, sometimes because the Italian sentries helped themselves to our rations, but often because an old sweat had "wangled" more than his share. We organised the issue of food very carefully, but even so we often had trouble. The situation was made more difficult by the fact that our numbers were never the same but constantly increasing.

The French soldiers had plenty of money, and since there are many French in Tunis, they bribed the sentries to let the Arabs sell them cakes and wine. They then kept what they wanted and sold the rest to the other P.O.Ws. I loved these wog cakes as we called them but had no money to buy them, but some officers had and we shared everything, so I got one or two. One was too hungry to wonder how the cakes were made.

I think most of us who were smokers missed our fags even more than food. I know I used to dream of Players blue boxes of 50 cigarettes. The men would give almost anything for them, and the Italian sentries took every advantage of the fact. In spite of our efforts to stop it, the men would exchange pull-overs, shirts, almost anything for food and cigarettes.

There were few attempts to escape. But one morning we entered the machine room in which there was a gantry crane; this had been pushed over so that one could climb up it to a trap door in the roof. This door was nailed up so the attempt was not a success and merely caused a sentry to fire into the room when he heard the noise of the moving gantry. The owner of the factory set up a storm of protest when he saw his precious gantry tipped up on its side, though quite undamaged. The Italians threatened to stop all food until the perpetrator owned up, which he did forthwith; and agreed to pay for the damage after the war. What a farce!

We were fed in the large room which overlooked the street. We used to stand by the barred windows and watch the passers-by. Many gave us the V. sign. Many laughed at us and several people swore at us. One French woman used to go past every day with a little girl and two boys. They always smiled at us and unobtrusively gave us the V. sign. I was certain she would hide us if only we could escape. But the chance never came. Nearly all the French seemed to be pro British and were not afraid to show it. So the exasperated Italians put a sentry on the windows to keep us away.

Such was our life, we had no books to read, no chairs to sit on, our beds were straw on a cement floor. We spent our time sitting in the sun and yearning. It was then that I heard about the "Wogs" (i.e. Arabs). Both armies hated them but especially 1st Army. They robbed the wounded and dead, spied on the British; and many a British prisoner who succeeded in escaping was caught by the Arabs and handed over to the Germans. Some of the stories of their revolting cruelty to prisoners were unbelievable. But though possibly exaggerated, they were not entire romances. Both armies took to laying booby traps by their unburied dead to prevent pillage.

Ian English came in about three days after I did; he was captured in the first attack on the Mareth Line and his news though not pessimistic rather dashed our hopes of release by the 8th Army.

Then one evening the Italians asked for the Padre who acted as our interpreter since both he and the "Ites" could speak French. He returned with the news that we were moving at dawn the next morning. Several futile attempts at escape were made. Many of us [sought] a hiding place in order that we might be left behind. But it was of no use, and on April 4th I think it was we left that factory.

We were driven down to the harbour in lorries, very early in the morning; we were closely guarded and the lorries travelled fast, but the worst blow was that though it was early the streets were swarming with Wops and Jerries. [German enemy]

We were split into two lots for two different ships and though we did not realise it then the first lot was destined for the best P.O.W. camp in Italy and the second for one of the worst. I was in the second lot.

Our ship was the "Forte De France" – she was little larger than a cross Channel boat (e.g. The Maid of Orleans) but looked fairly modern and used oil fuel. In our party there were 13 officers and about 350 other ranks. We were all put into the hold and told that if we gave any trouble we should be battened down. Later in the day the officers were allowed up on deck; we asked that the men might be allowed up also. The request was refused.

The men were only allowed up singly for the purposes of nature. Since there was only [accommodation] for 3 men at a time, for these purposes, throughout the voyage there was an everlasting queue for the latrines; to make matters worse the men being very hungry drank far too much water to try and ease the pangs of hunger, and as a result were constantly wanting to relieve themselves. As there were over 300 of them and latrine accommodation for only 3 men at a time, and as many of them were still suffering from dysentery, one can imagine the trials they had to endure.

When the officers first came up on deck we were moving slowly out of Tunis harbour, the sun was up and warm, the sea outside the harbour a deep and shiny blue, broken by countless brilliant white horses, which sprang into view and then were lost again only to reappear elsewhere. In the harbour the water was green, almost yellow in places and smelt of rotting seaweed. Behind us Tunis looked cleaner and whiter than we knew it to be and the white houses and domes stood out sharply against the hills behind them. It looked very peaceful and except for a very distant mutter every now and then, it sounded peaceful too. Then one looked at the harbour and the illusion of peace was smashed. Docks and cranes and ships and buildings were one bewildering mass of rubble in one part of the harbour. Here and there a ship's funnel could be seen staring out of the sea, here a ship leant drunkenly against the remains of a wharf, there a crane had fallen onto a ship and was perched on the concertinaed funnels like a hen on a vast egg.

Several docks and berths had not been damaged at all and were humming with activity but those that had been bombed were quite deserted and no effort had been or was being made to repair the damage.

We remained near the harbour entrance all that day and night. At night we slept in the hold with the men – it was very hot and very stuffy, and we were so crowded that it was a work of art to find space to lie on.

Before going to sleep we had a sing-song to keep our spirits up. I slept fitfully; the latrine procession continued and as I was near the ladder I was frequently trodden on. Judging by the language I was not the only sufferer.

The next morning the officers were again allowed on deck and again we requested that the men should be allowed up as well. The Italian Captain refused, we persisted and he became excited and lost his temper. (All Italians lose their tempers on the slightest provocation and behave like childish idiots.) We laughed at his stupidity and he threatened to shoot us, and told the sentry that he knew what his rifle was for and to use it without hesitation. We told the Captain that we should report his conduct to the Protecting Power. Hatred is an unpleasant but very real emotion and I have never felt it so strongly as I did for that Wop.

We left Tunis at 0900 hrs. and then beheld an amazing sight, flying very low came JU. 52ˢ [Junkers aircraft] by the hundred and savoyas [Savoia aircraft] as well, we reckoned their numbers at 750–1000. They were obviously bringing supplies. How we longed to see the R.A.F. but they did not appear; (I learnt later that this daily air supply service was interrupted by the R.A.F. and over 90 of the planes were shot down).

Our convoy of 2 ships and 2 destroyers was escorted by a flying boat. The destroyers were Italian; they looked fast and sea worthy, but whereas on a British destroyer you can hardly move a yard without tripping over a gun, these hardly seemed to have a gun on them and no "multiple pom-poms" [Royal Navy 2-pounder, anti-aircraft, 40mm canon] at all.

On our own ship we only had light ack ack [anti-aircraft guns] manned by German marines, who though they were our enemies, had one thing in common with us – scorn and loathing of the Wops.

A young Italian Tenante (Subaltern) was in charge of us. He was scared stiff of the crossing, and seemed equally frightened of both the Captain and ourselves. He could speak appallingly bad French and so could we and we did our best to understand one another. He offered one of us a cigarette and was promptly surrounded by 12 other officers, hence that gesture cost him 15 cigarettes. He told us he had been a journalist in peace time; he hated war, loathed the Germans and only wanted the thing to finish. He did what he could for us and the men, but was too frightened to be of any real use.

Our rations now consisted of two hard but large dry biscuits (very like dog biscuits minus meat) and half a tin of Italian bully [Bully Beef, i.e. Corned Beef] (a whole tin would have made a decent dinner for one man) and that was all.

We noticed that the Captain always wore a large scarlet life jacket. I never saw him without it. It was not the "Mae West" type but resembled a 'lilo' worn like a waistcoat. He was a short stumpy little man and he looked like a "Michelin motor tyre" advertisement. The crew had no life jackets; but they wore their boots without laces, and their clothes unbuttoned in case of emergency. If we were torpedoed we had little hope but we knew that our subs [submarines] concentrated on convoys approaching Africa and ships departing from Africa were usually left alone; and so we could only hope for the best.

We were on that ship for 5 days and 4 nights and got to know the crew quite well. Although we were allowed on deck, we had to remain aft and were not allowed to come forward at all. Thus we were very near the crew's quarters and we soon found out that they were a very mixed lot. All of them had been forced aboard ship, since the pay was insufficient to lure them to face the perils of the British subs and planes. All of them loathed Mussolini. But were frightened to tell us so if they thought they would be overheard.

One of them – an engine greaser (SALVADORE was his name) – had lived in New York and could speak a little English and he was magnificent, he was small, grey-haired, ugly and far from clean but cheerful and kind. He pinched, begged and borrowed food for us; now a loaf, then a piece of cheese and so on. Every time we methodically divided it into 13 and solemnly ate it. A mouthful if we were lucky.

The Ward room steward also got us what he could, in fact one morning he gave us some coffee but was "ticked off" by the Captain for doing so.

One of the deck hands was a Czech, showed us his hand – his trigger finger was 'off' down to the middle joint. He told us he shot it off to avoid having to fight for the Tedesci (Germans). His wife and parents had been transported to Germany and he had no news of them. He gave us what few cigs etc. he could spare. We mentioned Mussolini and he spat and made a great show of cutting his throat. He loathed the Croats as well and one could see in his bitterness and hatred, the typical attitude of the quarrelsome Baltic states. "Russia come to us from the North", he said, "You from the South and the sooner the better."

Another deck hand was an out and out crook, seeing us all desperately hungry he tried to get watches, rings etc. for the food that we longed for. We warned the men about him, but I know he got several watches. I thought of the army watch I had on me, it was broken and if I was searched it would be taken. I let him have it for cigarettes and bread, which I shared with my own men and the other officers. I was very proud of my own chaps, they behaved splendidly throughout and were always cheerful.

The last three nights on board five of us officers slept in a pokey little room that the crew used by day, there was just room for me to lie full length on the table, but if the motion of the ship increased much I was in danger of sliding off, but at least it was better than the hold. One night we were so squashed that I crept outside in a small passage and lay down there and the sentry promptly tripped over me, but lent me a blanket to lie on; so that was worthwhile.

Every day we begged, flattered, threatened, asked, demanded and requested that the men might be allowed on deck, that they should be given more rations and better latrine facilities. Each time we were refused, or worse still, promises were made and forgotten.

I think it was April the sixth that we first sighted land on the starboard side and the crew told us we were heading for Naples, then said we had passed Naples and were making for Livorno. The latter surmise was correct and we docked that evening. We were all delighted at the prospect of leaving the ship and spending a night anywhere but in the hold or crew room.[1]

But having run up the Quarantine Flag (a yellow penant) nothing more happened and we had to spend yet another night on board.

Next morning the men were at last allowed on deck and we were counted and counted again. One man on board had been wounded and the healed wound broke open (in his hand and arm). The crew had treated him well and he was now taken off to hospital. At last we left the ship and were escorted to a bath house in the docks. There we all had a bath, our clothes were disinfested and the men's heads were clipped till they were all as bald as billiards balls. This caused much loud laughter and the shower baths made us feel new men again; the officers' communal razor (we had shared one razor and 3 blades for nearly a fortnight) acquired a new blade and we all felt better but ravenously hungry.

A sergeant in the Grenadier Guards started to talk to me but I could not stand it; he had a friend who was chief chef at the Criterion, and was constantly telling me how he used to visit him and was allowed into the kitchens and invited to partake of any dish that pleased him. I had listened to this sergeant with a watering mouth too often on that ship and could not endure it further. I told him so and he laughed, "What about roast turkey now, sir?" "Go away", I replied. Whilst on that subject I might say that the chief chef apparently takes orders from nobody, even the manager cannot order him about in his kitchen; furthermore he is a very rich man, gets a £10 Tip at least from every participant in a big dinner, and in this way may earn anything up to £200 in one evening.

While we were waiting for the men to finish bathing, I and several other officers had a normal haircut; the barbers were pleasant fellows and one of them had sung as an extra in opera. We asked him to sing to us; he was very pleased to do so and sang the "Ave Maria" and several Italian songs; he had a beautiful tenor voice. Arnie Vivian could also sing very well so he joined in, the barber looked a little hurt, he obviously preferred singing on his own, but he recovered himself and carried on for nearly an hour.

When we left the ship we had been handed over to an Italian Captain, he was tall, well made, fair headed and thank goodness quiet and not excitable. He promised us our day's ration which we had not yet had and

---

[1]   That Evening Macdonald Smith (who should have been on the other ship) left us and joined the other party.

eventually they arrived. This time we got 1 loaf and a whole tin of Italian Bully each.

I should have mentioned that the last two days on board ship, our meagre rations had to be still further cut down amongst the officers; as we had a fixed amount for the voyage and some had been stolen. We suspected the Italian sentries and I am also sorry to say two Warrant Officers. By our going short, the men got their full ration until the last day when they too had to share two tins of meat between 5 men. There was nearly a very nasty row then; and the job of getting the men into lots of 5 in a dark and crowded hold, and giving each 5 their ration, was very hard especially as several scroungers tried to come twice for their rations. Discipline was maintained but only just – one realises the importance of discipline in times like these.

To resume – it was now midday we had all had baths and were waiting for a train to take us to –? No one would tell us where we were going to. There must have been nearly 100 guards round us and we were able to walk about a bit. Livorno was a large port, there were masses of supplies there, including thousands of gallons of oil, ammunition and trucks. It had hardly been bombed at all (within 3 weeks it was knocked to blazes), one thing was very interesting – concrete gun emplacements, pill boxes and weapon pits were being hastily erected and we spoke to the workmen who were doing it. They were quite friendly, but could hardly understand what we said.

At last our train arrived and after a terrific to-do amongst our guards (orders, counter orders, disorder, pandemonium) we were conducted in small parties to our carriages.

The men were in 3rd class carriages and we were 2nd class, which meant that we had a softer seat than they did. After the boat, that train was almost like a drawing room sofa as regards comfort. Our guards remained outside on both sides of the train. There were over a hundred of them, i.e. about 1 guard for every three prisoners.

Suddenly the train started to move, the guards rushed onto the train and we moved off for 300 yards. Then stopped for some time but at last we were well and truly started. Ted Edwards and I ate half our food and lay back in comfort smoking some fag ends that still remained to us. Ted lifted one foot on to my seat and yawned. "Quite comfortable at last", he said and closed his eyes.

One of the guards in the Carabinieri who was in the corridor shouted at him gesticulating wildly. Ted opened his eye. "Go away you silly little man," he said. The Guard seized Ted's leg and tried to force it off my seat. "Oh that's the trouble eh? Listen you filthy little – ite, take your hands off me." Ted was a policeman in Peace Time and though he could not speak Italian he spoke such rich, lurid and loud English that the guard must have gathered that he was slightly unpopular. Anyway he rushed off and returned with a young officer, rather a dandy, and very aggressive.

He threatened various things; Ted moved his erring boot and told him in a mixture of French, English and Italian that he would have done so at once if he had been asked to do so sensibly. To this the little dandy made a long and heated reply, and I became annoyed and when he had finished I merely said "No Compri." This caused a terse rejoinder and out he went, amid laughter from the others. "What did he say?" I asked.

Ted grinned "He says that if we do not behave as gentlemen we shall not be treated as such, and to you he said that if you don't understand you will soon be made to do so."

"Is he our example of the gentleman," asked someone else.

"Yes! Let's ask him."

"Oh leave the little un alone and let's have some peace." This latter piece of advice was accepted.

We were now flying through the Italian countryside. I was struck by the large number of trees that I saw, and yet there were hardly any woods or copses. But poplar trees were growing all over the place; the fields all contained at least six trees in them, dotted about all over the place singly; seldom in clumps. The country was either dead flat or mountainous, never undulating as in England. Most of the poplars are of course nurses to the vines, but even so there seemed to be no end to them. The farming was very crude, ploughing by oxen with a ramshackle single furrow plough. So much I could see from the train but I cannot now remember that journey very well.

We stopped in Rome at about midnight and at about 10 o'clock next morning we drew up at Capua. Having travelled south for nearly 200 miles, we were now near Naples and could see Vesuvius from the train. Of this date I am quite certain. On Friday 9 April 1943 we arrived at "CAMP CONCENTRAMENTO PRIGIONIERO DE GUERRA, No.66" as the camp was called.

We marched out of the station and in about ten minutes we reached the camp. The other ranks left us for a different part of the camp and we were conducted to the "Orderly Room."

"Good morning Gentlemen. If you will step in here, I will fix you up as soon as I can. Welcome to Capua Gentlemen, I expect you are wanting a cigarette?" Thus did R.S.M. [Regimental Sergeant Major] Burgess – of the Cheshires [The Cheshire Regiment] greet us. It did one good to see him, his boots polished and shining, his shorts and khaki drill as clean and smart as if he were on his own regimental barrack square. He made the Italian soldiers and Carabinieri look like so many recruits dressed as scarecrows. The R.S.M. gave us each a cigarette and told us to prepare for a search, in the meantime he noted down the name etc. of each officer. An Italian orderly who was present advised us to hide knives and compasses if we had any as they would certainly be taken from us. I asked the R.S.M. if there had been many escapes; he grinned "Many attempts Sir." We sent another Vatican telegram to our homes.

The search was not very thorough. I possessed a magnetic collar stud which I put in my mouth; it was not discovered. After the search we were marched into the officers' compound of the camp. There were the usual questions, several officers discovered friends in the camp and there was a long and animated exchange of greetings and experiences.

The camp consisted of 5 or 6 compounds each consisting of some half dozen huts and each completely surrounded by barbed wire; around the whole camp ran another barbed wire fence. It was chilly and wet when we arrived and the whole place looked very depressing, muddy, dirty and uncomfortable. Behind the wire the inmates reminded one irresistibly of animals in a zoo. Small stoves roughly made of tins smoked around each hut; the inmates were attired in varying forms of dress, some had shorts, others trousers, some wore beards and all looked rather bored and depressed.

However when we had been marched in our spirits rose. We split up into syndicates and Ted Edwards and I agreed to share together with Ian English and Scotty White. We drew iron bedsteads and boards to put on some palliasses, sheets (what luxury?) and a couple of blankets each. Some fellows instead of choosing boards for their beds, chose a canvas sheet which was hung from the bedstead by iron hooks; though these canvas sheets made a softer couch, they also harboured bugs – I was informed – so I chose the harder bed. While talking to our new acquaintances and making my bed, Perry Green offered me a cup of tea. Tea! My word it was good. I looked around me – clearly I must learn to use my hands – officers were making stoves out of tins, shelves from Red Cross Boxes, cupboards, even rough tables – all somewhat crude and rough but, as I soon discovered, all very necessary.

We then received our Red Cross Parcels, Ted and I were to share one, it was to last us until the following Monday (it was then Friday) we also received 50 cigarettes each and they had to last us until the Monday week. The parcel like most of those of the Canadian Red Cross contained 1 tin butter and 1 marmalade, a large bar of chocolate, a packet of raisins, of tea, of sugar and of salt. A tin of bully beef, salmon, sardines and Klim, and a packet of prunes. Ted and I were delighted. "Klim" we discovered was milk powder, the tin in which it arrived was the largest tin one ever got and consequently highly useful. Finally the parcel contained 1 bar of soap.

Ted and I were so hungry that we immediately ate the "Italian Bully" that remained to us from the journey. We were given our daily bread issue, which consisted of a small loaf each, shaped like a miniature Zeppelin and 200 grammes in weight.

Scarcely had we finished our meal when there was a shout of "Dinner up" and we followed the officers into another hut known as the "Mess". As we entered a few of the flies were good enough to go, but many remained. I was allocated a place and given a stool to sit on. At my table I found, Colin Leslie, John Wiggin, Lord Brabo[u]rne and Arnie Vivian. As Lord Brabo[u]rne was the only one who was not a newcomer, he spent most of the meal answering questions. The table was partially covered by an old table cloth and the meal consisted of a sort of stew of macaroni and cabbage and plenty of water. Followed by fresh lettuces and small fish which were far from fresh. After dinner all the new arrivals saw the Adjutant of the compound Pat Weir, and the S.B.O. (Senior British Officer) Major Webb, they told us how the camp was run and so on. We then returned to our hut and found most of the inmates asleep. I was strongly advised to make a stove; I wandered outside in search of some spare tins and discovered the W.Cs and Wash House. In the former all the wooden seats and many of the window frames had been removed obviously for firewood. The wash house consisted of about ten basins and two stone troughs large enough to wash one's clothes in, but not one's body. Many of the basins were a dirty grey colour owing to the large number of fire blacked tins that had been washed therein. Outside the wash house I discovered a crate of dirty tins, a refuse pit and several thousand flies. Somewhat disconsolately I searched for the inevitable Klim tin with which to construct a stove. My luck was in and I bore it off in triumph and washed it; a wire handle had been fitted to it and I decided to use it as a saucepan.

It was then that I noticed several Italian workmen; they were removing the roofing felt from our hut and putting up corrugated asbestos. They were anxious to keep the wooden slats that had been used to hold down the felt; we were even more anxious to obtain some for firewood and most of us managed to get a fair supply. One officer was chased round the hut by an irritated workman, and while he was away we all took what we could.

At about 2.30 (dinner was at 11) we all queued up for boiling water and made tea therewith. Ted and I had our tea in Italian issue mugs which were made of aluminium and extremely difficult, thanks to their shape, to drink out of. On looking round we discovered that the old inhabitants had made themselves mugs out of tins. Porridge tins from English parcels were best, and the handles, some of which were very cleverly made, were constructed out of other tins.

Our evening meal at 4.30 was much the same as before – we also had one apple each. At about 7.30 we obtained more boiling water and at 11.30 the lights were put out; I was advised to make my bed early, for if there were an air raid, all the lights in the camp were extinguished.

During the evening meal Major Webb announced that the Italian workman complained that a P.O.W. had taken a pair of pliers; if they were not returned there would be a search. (Groans). The major asked for the return of the pliers, and Bettel blushingly gave them to him, amid loud laughter.

Thus ended my first day at Capua, I went to bed in a pair of pants in lieu of pyjamas. The room was slightly heated by two small electric stoves balanced on a precarious erection of stools, each stove was surrounded by a motley collection of tins containing, biscuit or real porridge or perhaps a night cap of cocoa or tea. I slept fitfully and thankfully; it was only a transit camp and hence a little rough and ready but compared to Tunis and the ship it was heaven.

I have dwelt at some length on such subjects as Tunis, food and homemade stoves, firewood and other things both mean and petty. For at that time such petty things as these were our major problems. We had sufficient food but far less than we had previously been accustomed to receive in the army and consequently we always felt hungry. In fact I freely confess it took me a long time to become accustomed to P.O.W. fare. Razors and razor blades were very hard to obtain, shaving soap was a luxury; amongst the new arrivals none of us had towels, tooth brushes nor a change of clothes, not even socks. We used the material from our field dressings as towels; and handkerchiefs were used for the same purpose. While we were at Capua we obtained tooth brushes, razors and even shaving soap and mirrors through the canteen. While the Red Cross provided us with shirts, pullovers, socks and underwear as issued by the British Army but all this took a long time.

As the weather was very warm I decided to make a pair of shorts out of an army shirt; I purchased some Italian needles and thread and set to work. Italian needles are delicate and brittle and I broke several, the thread was coarse and broke very easily. The job took me about a month as I often gave up in disgust. When I tried them on as I frequently did, there was always uproarious laughter. John Canning in particular was literally reduced to tears.

Every morning the flies woke one up, buzzing round one, crawling over one's face, into one's ears even up one's nostrils. We used to swat them, trap them and at sight kill hundreds with burning tapers, but it made no difference, there were always thousands of them.

We used to do P.T. [physical training] each morning before breakfast; breakfast consisted of hot coffee supplemented by the contents of our parcels. Roll call was then held in a pleasantly informal method, and the rest of the day was at our disposal, as already described. The Italians would count us again during the meal.

For the first few days, Ted and I were busy making ourselves as comfortable as possible; Ted soon showed himself as an excellent, if somewhat short-tempered cook and we soon settled down. We wrote home one week after our arrival, April 15; we used to get one letter card and one postcard each week.

As regards pay; we had to prove our rank i.e. get someone who knew us to acknowledge in writing that we were Captain – Lts etc. The exchange rate was 70 Lira to the £ and the few goods in the canteen were very expensive, and in such demand that they usually had to be bought on a rosta system.

The most enjoyable amusement at Capua were the walks, which were held about twice a week, half of us going each time. It was a great relief to get away from the barbed wire and though we were made to march in 3s closely escorted by sentries, in spite of the fact that we were on parade, yet it gave one a sense of freedom. We used to walk out to a little village nearby and visit an old chapel there situated about 200 feet up in the hills with a glorious view of the flat plain surrounding Capua. This plain stretched to the sea and inland was bounded by a vast semicircle of mountains and hills. From the chapel we could see Vesuvius with a thin plume of smoke above it. Thanks to the volcanic ash the land is extraordinarily fertile; grapes, oranges, lemons and cherries, apples, peaches grew in profusion; such space as was not occupied by fruit trees was thick with corn up to the fruit trees themselves. Luxuriant fodder crops were being gathered in crude carts by children, women and a few old men. Odd patches of land were being ploughed by means of ancient single furrowed implements drawn by oxen. The roads were dusty, rough and carried little but farm traffic and bicycles.

On one other walk we used to go to the "Mineral Springs" a delightful, sleepy country spot; the springs themselves were clear and brilliantly coloured, but the water tasted foul – sulphur and bad eggs. On nearly all these walks the weather was glorious and our escorting guards in their thick and heavy uniforms looked with envy at our thin shirts, shorts and open collars. The local inhabitants took little interest in us but were often openly impudent to our guards. One imp of a boy yelled some remark to the escorts as we marched through the village and was promptly given a hearty "clip over the ear". At first we used to sing on the walks, but "Tipperary" was too popular with the people; especially those who remembered the last war; hence it was forbidden. We noticed various gun positions were being dug in the hills overlooking the Volturno, and the bridge over that river was already prepared for demolition – a hopeful sign.

In the camp there was little to do beyond scrounging wood, washing such clothes as we had and similar domestic functions. There were very few books and a high demand for them. We had Italian newspapers and by means of these kept fairly up to date with the news. The barber who was a soldier and came daily, used to tell us a little more news and the sentries were discretely and judiciously 'pumped' whenever we had the chance.

The other ranks' compound next to ours contained the chaps who were captured with me and we used to talk to each other across the wire. This was forbidden but the sentries were usually too lazy to do anything about it. But if the conversation went on for too long, the sentry would open and close the bolt of his rifle and point the thing at us. We would then give him a cigarette and go on talking or if cigarettes were short as they were normally, the conversation would cease.

The Italian sentries had a great weakness for tea and would swop fresh eggs for it. This market was however soon closed because the O.Rs ingeniously threw tins over to the Wops with fresh tea at the top and dust and mud underneath. They would also dry 'used' tea leaves in the sun and "flog" this to the Wops.

There were several concert parties, which the O.Rs put on and were much enjoyed. Richard Garrett also produced several "radio plays".

Before I arrived, a wholesale attempt at escape was made by the other ranks. It failed through poor control. This is what happened. One man discovered a manhole cover and as he was out of the sentries' view, he managed to lift it and disclosed a vast sewer, practically dry. He promptly got down into it, immediately others followed and the sentry then spotted them and shouted for the "carabinieri". These gentlemen dashed out of the camp into a field into which the sewer led. The other carabinieri covered the entrance to the sewer and 15 men were caught inside it – none escaped. The men were hopelessly trapped but the carabinieri, as if for spite, fired up the sewer and three men were injured and I think one was killed.

While I was at the camp, there was another tragedy. A working party of O.Rs had gone to the station to collect some Red Cross parcels that had arrived. Two escaped, the countryside was searched and they were found and surrounded. Realising they were caught they put up their hands and walked over to the "Carabinieri", who promptly shot them in cold blood, one was killed and the other badly wounded. It was ironical when the dead man was given a military funeral in the camp.

There was little to do in the camp as I have already said, but we used to have a "Brains Trust" and various lectures. Padre Collins gave a splendid lecture on the Boat Race. He rowed for Cambridge for 3 years. Others were "The Whaling Industry", "Tea and Planting", "Archery" and "Association Football".

In spite of all our efforts the boredom became oppressive and I longed to get to a permanent camp. We organised a sports meeting with such facilities as were available; a race meeting was also held and bridge became more and more popular. Auction sales of food for cigarettes on parcel days.

Before leaving Capua I must describe a few more of its inmates. There were about 30 French officers there. Some from the Foreign Legion and some from North African regiments. They were popular and knew how to look after themselves. Their little clay cooking ovens were masterpieces and one of them was in great demand at all concerts. They loathed the Italians and caused some trouble one night by throwing stones at a sentry whose vocal efforts disturbed their sleep. The camp was of course floodlit but all the light shone onto the barbed wire, hence the French were in shadow and the unfortunate sentry could not see them. Many of the French were repatriated evidently to conciliate them and I heard that several went back to Africa via Spain and fought again.

Major Webb was the S.B.O. A New Zealander and a schoolmaster he gave several splendid lectures, notably the Campaigns in Greece and

Crete. He was an excellent fellow, but it was vulgarly and truly said of him that he had "Verbal Diarrhoea".

Philip Kindersley[2] was the leading humourist, his lecture on Horse Racing was magnificent. I discovered that he knew Arthur Marchant slightly. Art Smedly was an American, he slept next to me. He was shot down over Galrs [?] and was badly burnt about the face; it healed well but the sun burnt the tender skin and showed up his old burn and even the marks of his goggles were visible by the flesh being whiter than the rest of his sunburnt face. He used to have a terrific pudding one day with a friend of his, they would spend the next day in bed with stomach ache, and the following day they would have another rich pudding and so it went on. There were several other Americans there and we had many discussions with them. Several fellows were getting letters from home but Ted and I were due for a long wait in that respect.

Air raids were numerous at night; and then all the lights including the flood lighting of the wire would go out and the alarm would be sounded on the bugle. We would cheer and laugh when we heard this alarm, but the sentries' trigger fingers always seemed to itch; rifles would go off for no apparent reason but no one was ever hit.

Just before we left there was a big daylight raid; we could see hundreds of big four-engined bombers flying high over the camp evidently towards Rome. Nothing interfered with them, not even ack ack. This and the news of the fall of Tunis raised our spirits a great deal. More and more Germans were seen on the roads outside the camp. The Wops hated them – "Tedesci Pah" they would spit.

In about the middle of May, many officers left for Camp 49 and we had far more room as a result. One of the doctors who could speak Italian started classes in the language and I attended them. Then the French officers left and also the Americans so that there were only about 10 of us left. But more prisoners soon arrived; bringing news of big raids on Naples harbour in which an ammunition ship had been hit and blown up with such violence that it did more damage than the bombs themselves. Rumours were rife: "Invasion of Sicily, of France, of Germany, of Greece." Rumours of air raids and so on and so forth.

Amongst the new arrivals was a Major and 2 Subalterns of the – Regt. They had attempted to escape in Africa, while being driven back by

---

[2]   Hon. Philip Leyland Kindersley (1907-1995), author of *For You The War is Over*.

a German escort. They stopped for the usual purpose; the officers then knocked out the single German guard and bolted to a nearby wood where the Arabs promptly caught them and handed them back to Jerry. Now that sentry was badly hurt and before handing the officers over to the Ites the Bosch took all their particulars. The sequel took place at Capua, the camp was visited by a German officer who identified the three escapees and arranged that the Italians should hand them over to the Germans for trial by court martial. Then rumour started again; the German sentry had died and the officers were charged with murder. The Major who had actually struck the sentry, became nervous and hysterical, in fact he had a break-down; how much was genuine we did not know, but he was obviously a sick man when he and his subalterns were handed over to the Germans. We heard afterwards that the sentry was not dead, but even so they were in a very embarrassing position.

Then on about 28 May we were told that we were moving to a perma-nent camp. So many were going in one party to 49, the rest to No. 47. No one knew where the camps were or what they were like. Provided the right numbers were obtained for each camp, the Italians did not mind who went where. There was much discussion as to which camp was the better; Majoné the interpreter (employed by Cook's Tours in peace time) could give us no information about either. Parties for each camp were organised and then disintegrated; changes were made and counter changes until Major Webb, who had the thankless task of listing the two parties, became justifiably annoyed. Ted and I were torn between (a) going with our old acquaintances from Tunis to 49 and (b) going with our new acquaintances to 47. Little did we know then how much depended on our decision. We were listed to go to 49 but at the last moment we changed our minds in order to get away from a certain gentleman who "got on our nerves".

On 31 May we left Capua. Such baggage and food as we had was searched by the Carabinieri – the search was laughably inefficient. Forbidden articles were handed to friends by the "patients" before being searched and recovered afterwards. One officer who intended to escape had some Italian money for that purpose; he proudly displayed it after the search saying "I had no difficulty in getting this through", when a Carabinieri guard spotted him and confiscated the lot. We left the camp in the afternoon waving and shouting to the O.Rs and few remaining officers. Carrying our ungainly Red Cross Parcels containing food and spare clothing we marched in threes to Capua station. There were many Germans in the town, nearly all of them being "Hermann Goerings."

I wondered if they were the same Division as those who had captured me in Africa. But it seemed unlikely. We waited for some time at the station, there were crowds of civilians there, all tried to see us and many spoke to us though the officer in charge of us tried to prevent them doing so. There were some German A/A trucks in a siding but little else of importance.

Eventually our train arrived and we settled into our second class carriages. As usual there were crowds of guards who lined up on either side of the train. When we started there were several guards in the corridor and one in each compartment. On the journey northwards I was struck by the Italian gardens, nearly all of them grew wheat or maize actually in the garden itself. At first the country was flat and uninteresting, we could only see flat fields and vineyards with the grapes trained to elm, lime or poplar trees. I was disappointed. We reached Rome at about midnight and waited there for nearly two hours. The next day the train travelled northwards and the country became more and more hilly. The railway passed through numerous tunnels, over embankments, bridges and through cuttings, as hill and valley followed each other in swift succession. "If we invade Italy we shall have a hard time in these hills", someone remarked, "Yes, it is like North Africa, only worse", replied another.

By midday on 1 June we had reached Bologna and there we remained for nearly three hours. Here the civilians were most interested. We stopped under a bridge that carried a road over the railway. Crowds of people passed over it and many stopped to look down on us; some of them threw us cigarettes which our perspiring guards obligingly collected and gave to us. A little Italian Officer on the train was obviously annoyed; he came down the corridor, bawled at his sentries and tried to make us get into our compartments; as he went he pulled down the blinds in the corridor and as he passed we let them up again and carried on our sign language with the civilians on the bridge. The little Ite Officer got more and more furious; seeing Taffy's beard he threatened to pull it. Taffy put out his chin, "Go on, try", he said. It was just as well for all of us that the Officer decided that "discretion was the better part of valour."

Eventually we left Bologna and arrived at Modena at about 1700 hrs. Here we detrained, got into lorries and were driven to the camp. Though several fellows in our party had decided to try and escape, they had not done so; in their plans they had not reckoned on having a sentry actually in the compartment.

When we reached the camp we were astounded. It was a large enclosure surrounded by a brick wall, about eight feet high with several strands of barbed wire along the top of it. Compared to Capua it was enormous, all the buildings were of brick and not wood, though all were single storey buildings. Actually it had been a barracks, built within the last few years. They were large, clean and airy; and were built to enclose a large rectangle which was used for parades, sports etc. When we arrived we were again searched – thoroughly – during the search an orderly brought us tea. He himself was searched before leaving. We all had to strip to our birthday suit and our baggage was carefully examined. David Rolls and others provided much entertainment; Italian money was discovered on them in all the likely hiding places which the searchers knew perfectly. All sorts of forbidden articles appeared from their kit and clothing. The Italians said little but now and again permitted themselves a smile. Eventually we moved inside the camp itself through the inevitable barbed wire. Everyone appeared to be throwing balls about; tennis balls, cricket balls, footballs and baseball balls whizzed and bounced in all directions.

We were met at the entrance by David Dale, the Camp Adjutant and escorted by him to the S.B.O.'s office. Here we did our best to prove our identity (the Ites and Bosch often sent spies in as P.O.Ws) and were carefully examined with regards to our experiences: we told them all about ourselves and all the news so far as we knew it, including details of the latest weapons used by the British Army etc. All this was later published for the edification and instruction of the camp.

We were then allotted rooms, bedding etc. all vastly superior to that at Capua: as the Camp was very full, Mould, Wright, Edwards R.C. and Davies [and I] found ourselves in a passage outside the main rooms, which we had to ourselves and contrived to make it reasonably comfortable.

We met Macdonald Smith and various others who had been at Tunis with us but left in a different ship and went to a different camp. They were better treated on board than we were and went to Camp 38 at POPI which was about the best in Italy.

In the evening we were given an excellent meal in the mess and we began to feel more and more optimistic. The camp looked magnificent. There were over a thousand officers there, commanded by Lt Col Shuttleworth (New Zealand). They were nearly all South Africans or New Zealanders – about 800 S.A., 300 N.Z. and 100 odd Englishmen including ourselves. Most of them had been captured in the fall of Tobruk and in the fighting preceding it, and had thus been P.O.Ws. for about one year. Others had been taken at Sidi Rezegh 8 months previous to the fall of Tobruk.

Our bungalow (No 6.) contained South Africans, and they were extremely good to us; by the time night came we all had towels, pyjamas, shirts and shaving kit. They besieged us for news and were very anxious to know what we in England thought of the fall of Tobruk. One and all they blamed their commander and all agreed that they could have either put up a much better fight for it or have got out altogether without losing many men or much equipment.

Many of them had fought in Abyssinia in which they defeated an enemy ten times as strong as themselves. Wheeler – a gunner – told me the Italians were so anxious to surrender that they were never in action for long. But they all expressed great admiration for the way in which the Italians had commenced to colonise the country. Their roads were excellent and their houses and sanitation arrangements were good; most of them went so far as to say that Abyssinia ought to be returned to the Italians after the war. The Abyssinians themselves were mostly untrustworthy, uncivilised and extremely dirty.

We soon made many friends and joined a sports club. That night we slept soundly feeling very pleased with our new abode.

The next day 2 June 194[3] was spent in getting acquainted with the place; we discovered a bank, a library, a canteen, a theatre, an advertising agency, classrooms and many other amenities.

I could write many pages on the excellence of these institutions but have not the space to do so. I must however mention the canteen and theatre which were in the same room separated by a large wall made of Red Cross boxes. The canteen had a marble counter as part of the building; thanks to patience, ingenuity and skill it resembled a luxurious English bar, advertisements humorously and beautifully executed adorned the walls, the lights were painted and decorated and on the theatre doorway a booking office complete with pretty girl had been built and painted. Forthcoming attractions were advertised with [caricatures] of the actors taking part. The theatre itself resembled very closely a small new theatre in England, even to the ventilator in the ceiling. And all this had been done with the packing cases and cardboard boxes in which our Red Cross stores arrived.

The mess was excellently run, all cookable food was taken from the Red Cross parcels before they were delivered to the individuals and these added to the Italian rations made up our meals. We also received grapes in large quantities – some good but mostly rather small, but very enjoyable for all that.

I started playing basketball and soon got the hang of it. It was very fast and in the hot sun one worked up a beautiful lather but washing facilities were good and one frequently had three baths a day – under the cold tap.

The various sports clubs competed against each other at basketball, soccer, touch rugger and baseball. Each club had several teams for each game; the first teams reached a very high standard. For individuals there were many courts for tenniquoits. All the nets and gear had again been made from Red Cross string etc., the balls being provided by the Y.M.C.A.

Education was not neglected, and though I was disappointed in that I could not study for my exams since all such studies were for New Zealand or S.A. degrees; I was amazed at the wealth of learning displayed. Shorthand, Law, Advertising, Economics, Music, Philosophy, Medicine, First Aid, Psychology, Physiology, Agriculture (all colonial), all modern languages European, as well as Africanse [sic], Latin and Greek. I commenced learning Italian and shorthand and soon discovered I could not do both as the times clashed. I therefore concentrated on shorthand and had completed the beginners course when we left for Germany.

It was curious or perhaps due to influence that in our passage we should all commence reading books on farming. Jack Wright was keen on it and asked no more than to get back to a small farm in Shropshire where he lived before the war. There he had kept a small pub and a few pigs and in a small way had done very well and been very happy. Perhaps it was due to him that we started reading A.G. Street, Francis Brett Young and Massingham, but other P.O.Ws say that it is a phase that everyone goes through. But there were many books in the library that I wanted to read and I spent most of my spare time in reading the above authors. I read many books of Dickens, Dorothy Sayers, E.A. Poe, Stevenson, Ingoldsby, and many others.

There were many forms of entertainment, a theatre show once a fortnight, a "big match", soccer or basketball nearly every evening; an orchestra, a dance band and lectures.

Every week we had a turn entitled "Words and Music" in which we were given a resumé of the weeks news from the Italian papers, the sentries and other sources, together with some hints and theories as to the progress of the war – this talk was always given by a S.A. Intelligence officer whose name, curiously enough was Dimbleby (no relation to the reporter). In addition an officer would give us a talk on any subject of interest; Ted gave an excellent talk on the London Policeman, Arthur

Duvine gave another on his tour in America re Tank Production and Tactics. Then the orchestra would play original compositions or classics. Pat Quirke wrote several excellent tunes, marches etc. Also Trevor Dyer (a Doctor – Pat was an orchestra conductor as a civvy [civilian] and a band master in the army) and Len Inskip. Their best effort was Schubert's Unfinished Symphony.

The music society also gave concerts at least one evening a week – usually violin and chamber music, a few songs and occasionally a full orchestra. The dance band used to play daily when we received our wine issue and sat about in groups in the shade of an open air washing house with a roof, but no side walls, supported on arched brickwork.

Finally we had one Exhibition of Arts and Crafts; as usual I was astonished at the high standards obtained with such crude and limited material. Many of the paintings were of the desert, some showing actions, others content with the desert and sky alone, there were some lovely effects. There were many excellent pictures of the camp itself and other P.O.W. camps. Portraits, pen and ink sketches, water colours, oils, pencil and pastel work. The handicrafts also reached a very high standard; one exhibit showed a brush, comb, mirror and nail file, in a case made from tins, wood etc. lying about in the camp.

When we had been there about a month Mike Davies went to hospital with jaundice and Cliff with stomach trouble; visiting days were Sundays and Thursdays. The hospital was a similar Bungalow to ours, inside the wire but out of bounds except as above. Our own M.Os ran it and most of their supplies came in special Red Cross parcels; they got very little from the Italians except news. The Italian Padre, an R.C. used to visit the hospital nearly every day, he could speak English and used to tell them the radio news, sometimes (so he said) English radio news, he was, however, very unreliable and the hospital was a 'hot-bed' of rumour.

Besides the weekly news review the news was typed out daily by the "Central news agency" and a copy pinned on the notice board in each bungalow. In addition, all rumours, gossip etc. and all public news received from home by letter were reported by individuals to the "Central news agency" who checked up on rumours before publishing. In this way rumours were checked and "news from home" became a weekly edition.

I heard many interesting stories at Modena and heard about the terrible hardships endured by the P.O.Ws (mostly O.Rs) who, after their capture at Tobruk had to march all the way to Benghazi; there they were handed over to the Italians and remained several weeks near Benghazi before being transported to Italy. Most of the officers were flown over to Italy direct from Tobruk. I met several however, mostly doctors who remained with the men. The water supply in Tobruk had been blown up and early on in the march several men went mad with thirst, some died. Their captors, the Germans were nearly as badly off, and treated them as well as could be expected under the conditions but when they eventually reached Benghazi, water trucks approached and before their eyes were bombed by British planes. Eventually they got water, but were handed over to the Italians who treated them abominably. Seeing the state the men were in the Italian sentries gave them water in return for valuables. They were put in some form of camp; food was very short and starvation and dysentery caused more deaths. The hospital accommodation and supplies were almost non-existent; many operations were performed without anaesthetics (this occurred in Italy as well). The M.Os did all they could, they had to prevent hungry men from swapping part of their meagre rations for cigarettes which shows how strong is the craving for tobacco, particularly under trying conditions. Eventually they set out for Italy, one ship was torpedoed, the Italians and some prisoners started to panic, but a German officer on board shot three Englishmen and 2 Italians, stopped the panic and the ship managed to make port. This action by the German was in no way brutal; by killing 5 men he saved hundreds. On the voyage out we had orders to shoot any man who started a panic – the most infectious disease on earth.

On about 20 June 'Pop' Hudson arrived from the 8th Army and gave us an excellent talk on his experiences. He stressed one point – in all previous campaigns in the desert, the tanks had been the dominant arm – under Montgomery, it was once more an infantry battle – tanks, guns etc. being used to get the infantry forward. He told the same story of treatment as a prisoner – German fighting troops were extremely kind to him (The 90th Light Div.); the second line troops were not so good and the Italians were worst of all.

At Modena the Italians treated us fairly well, they had much respect for the S.B.O. and did quite a lot for us, though they promised a lot more DOMANI (To-morrow which never comes). The Camp Commandant was quite a good fellow but terribly scared of his superiors; he was always ringing up Rome before acquiescing to our requests.

An Italian Commandant of a P.O.W. camp nearly always get the sack if one of his charges escapes. As the job is a comparatively 'cushy' one they do all they can to keep it. I was told that the previous commandant was very unpopular, there was nearly a riot on roll call parade due to some incident which occurred; he became so hated that the S.B.O. 'escaped' and the Commandant was sacked. The S.B.O. was soon caught again and deprived of his command, but he had achieved his object.

The invasion and final conquest of Sicily caused rejoicings and crowds round the news notice boards. Rumours of invasions of Italy were rife. More and more German transport passed by the camp on a railway which was within a stone's throw of our bungalow. The Russian news was also good. Everyone became more optimistic, but more impatient yet, the days dragged, rumours increased. At last on 3 September we received news of the invasion of Italy.

But I am going too fast, thirsty though we were for news, in our passage we were just as anxious for letters from home. Everyone seemed to be getting letters except us. John Wiggin got 26 in one day, at last on 26 July ours arrived. I got 6 letters that day. On the same day as the papers said "Italy smiled again", Mussolini was voted out at the Council meeting. All the newspapers turned Royalist the same day.

At about the same time, perhaps a little earlier a very fine effort was made to escape by two South Africans. A siding from the Rly [railway] served the camp. Red Cross consignments were shunted in their trucks on to this siding, whence they were removed by working parties under guard. These two officers made a large screen one side of which was painted so as to resemble the woodwork of a truck. They carried this screen rolled up under a great coat with their provisions etc. on one such working party. The truck was unloaded in the normal manner, the others offered cigarettes to the sentries and talked to them, while the two escapists erected their screen. Thus creating a truck with a false end. Unfortunately when the sentry looked in one of them moved and the startled sentry saw the "woodwork" of the truck ripple and sway. – "Three weeks in the cooler."

I cannot leave Modena without mentioning Handy & Co. They provided the whole of Bungalow 6 (about 200) with hot tea every morning. They had constructed a truly magnificent "Stoofa" which burnt cardboard fuel to such an effect that it must have produced over 10,000 half pints of tea while we were at Modena. This excellent service was provided free of charge; all one had to do was to produce the tea which was easy.

But the great delight of Modena was a negative one – no flies – hence little or no dysentery. The mosquitoes however were vicious and plentiful. Other trials were clouds of dust whenever a wind arose, which was often. The parade and sports grounds were only earth – no grass existed save in very small patches. They were very dusty.[3]

Air raids were frequent at night; the Italian bugle would blow the alarm, the flood lighting would be switched off and we would cheer and stay in our bungalow, as ordered. Usually there were a few shots at someone belting home after visiting friends in another bungalow. We had an excellent view of a daylight raid on Bologna by several squadrons of 6 engined bombers – Fortresses and Liberators. One was hit by ack ack, right above the camp, at a great height. We saw 1 then 2, then 3 and eventually 5 Parachutes plume out in the sky. And heard afterwards that the Germans and the carabinieri arrived at the same time to capture the prisoners. The carabinieri were armed so they eventually got them; they were not however brought to our camp. I spoke to F/O. [Flying Officer] Wolfe about parachute jumping; it is so cold at that height (above 25,000 ft) that you have to do a delayed opening so as to fall into warmer atmosphere as quick as possible otherwise you may die of cold or be badly frost bitten – especially in winter.

We heard of the invasion of Italy on September 3, prior to that, acts of sabotage or apparent sabotage were reported daily. I remember one week in which a large fire was reported every day of the week, the causes of these 7 fires were not known. But they were very widespread [in] Milan, Bologna, Rome and other towns.

On September 8 I was playing patience on my bed (we had no table) after supper when Mike came in with a shout, "Armistice" – "What again!" I wearily replied. But this time it was no rumour. I went outside the bungalow and saw a huge crowd of cheering officers at the entrance. I rushed down and joined the crowd – "What a row!"

Outside the main entrance, separated from us by barbed wire – was another crowd of Italian civilians, mostly girls cheering, laughing and shouting "Viva Inglesi."

Someone let us out of the inner gate and the whole crowd of us swarmed to the outer gate and through that out into the main road where we were surrounded by Italian girls and civilians who seeing that we were not hostile endeavoured to talk to us. The word came that the S.B.O. had ordered us back to camp; so we all trooped back. After the first flush of delighted surprise we began to think what was best to be done. The

---

[3]   The dust was occasionally laid by violent thunderstorms usually at night and accompanied by the finest display of lightning I have ever seen.

S.B.O. published orders that we were to remain in camp and not to escape without his permission. The rumours increased hourly – many of them were due to the Italian Padre – "British Troops had landed at La Spezia", "Parachutists at Bologna, we were to hang on until the British arrived", and so on and so forth. Since there was nothing definite to be done, a concert was organised, extra wine was issued and all made merry. Men were shaking hands all round, and one of the few Italian officers whom we liked was invited to join us. The rumours increased, the Brenner Pass was said to be in Allied hands and it seemed impossible that we should be sent to Germany. But there were many Germans about and we did not want to start any incidents with them; hence the importance of remaining in camp. Then we were told that a War Office Order had been received through secret but absolutely reliable channels, that we were not to escape but to remain in the camp. After a hectic night we went to bed; two chaps tried to escape in the night but after climbing the wall they found the sentry waiting for them.

I was up early the following morning, 10 September, and heard sounds of rifle and M.G. fire from Bologna direction. It sounded as though the rumour of the parachutists landing there might be correct. Actually I subsequently discovered this firing was the result of a German attack on the P.O.W. camp at Bologna. After breakfast the Italian sentries started deserting in quick succession; it was a ludicrous sight. The Italian soldier would go out through a side exit carrying a suitcase or bundle; he would cross the railway and then disappear into a small crop of maize; after about ten minutes he would reappear from the other side of the maize in civilian dress and proceed to run away as fast as he could. About a dozen deserted in this manner. One Italian officer ran after them in a futile attempt to make them return. Soon there were hardly any sentries left. Several P.O.Ws made good their escape and went to houses nearby. Some of them soon returned saying that the Italians would not have them for fear of the Germans. The Germans had taken over all stocks of food in shops and stores and the Camp Q.M. [Quartermaster] was unable to obtain our rations that day. That did not matter as we had plenty of food.

At about 10.30 we were visited by a German Officer[4] who merely made a few polite remarks, said that he was fed up with War and then

---

[4]   Few of us saw this officer as almost the whole camp attended a Thanksgiving service. All denominations attended and all forms of bigotry were forgotten. A Church of England Padre (Knight) and R.C. Padre jointly conducted the service.

left. This incident upset everyone; it looked as though the Germans meant to take over the camp. Many more people tried to escape but the Italian Q.M. now clothed in civilian dress persuaded most of them to wait. We yearned for some definite news. After lunch the S.B.O. addressed the whole camp – we might escape if we wished to do so but he advised us not to – the Germans were going to take over the camp so those who meant to go should go at once. "They have arrived Sir, the Bosch are here", shouted a voice; sure enough a German section had arrived and proceeded to patrol the wire. There were not enough of them to do the job properly and one side of the camp was entirely unguarded; and here a long queue of Ps.O.W. climbed the wall and vanished. Jack and I were sorely tempted to go too but after much deliberation we decided to take the S.B.Os advice. Particularly as some escapees again returned because the Italians refused to help them for fear of the Germans and because they were short of food.

Meanwhile all the Italians had deserted, Officers and O.Rs including the Commandant. More Germans arrived and the camp was now properly guarded once more. Though the Germans must have seen several chaps get out, it did not seem to worry them. A German Officer arrived and told us we should be shot if we approached to within 20 yards of the wire. He gave no indication as to what was going to happen to us. We all hoped that they merely intended to keep an eye on us while the German army withdrew from Italy – this now sounds foolish but on the information given to us by the Italians, it seemed the most likely state of affairs. The Camp linguists proceeded to engage the sentries in conversation, gave them cups of tea and cigarettes and tried hard to get information from them. But they knew little more than we did. They had recently arrived from Russia and told us about the awful conditions there. "What do you think of the Italians?" they were asked. "The same as the Russians think of you", was the reply.

That night two officers made a dash over the wall and though they were fired on we saw them no more so they evidently got away. Roughly 100 officers escaped that day out of 1200.

The next day 11 September. We were informed by the S.B.O., that we had "backed the wrong horse" and were going to be sent to Germany on the following day. The Germans then held a nominal roll call using an old and out of date list of names which the Italians had left behind. After two weary hours they gave it up and merely noted the total numbers of those present. We then were allotted into parties each being under command of one of our own majors. My party and several others were told to be ready to move at 3 o'clock next morning and were warned that we should have to carry our kit to the station – about 3 kilometres away.

We had now accumulated a considerable quantity of kit and an immense amount of food was in store which individuals were saving up for the winter when appetites were keener and rations shorter. There was then far more food in the camp than we could possibly carry, and rather than let the Germans have it, several bungalows started burning their surplus food and clothing. Large bonfires appeared in which unpierced tins exploded with considerable violence. Bangs! and pops were heard all over the place and clouds of smoke arose together with a reek of burning material and food. It reminded me of Dunkirk. Several of us thought this was a terrible waste and as we knew the Italian civilians were short of food we decided to throw our spare food over the wall. This would feed the hungry and no doubt cause the Italians to feel more kindly disposed towards us and so benefit those who had already escaped and assist those who might yet get away. Accordingly we all took tins of cheese, biscuits, butter etc. down to the end of our bungalow nearest the wall. We could see several girls and children on the railway embankment the other side of the wall not 30 yards from us.

Some bars of soap and a tin or two of cheese whizzed over the wall. The children shouted for joy and began collecting these remarkable gifts; then women and children rushed out of the houses near by shouting "Viva Inglesi". We signed to them to keep quiet and keep clear; then sent a perfect hail of stuff over the wall; cheese, klim, condensed milk, margarine, butter, jam, biscuits, egg flake, fruit, meat, vegetables and stews in tins of all shapes, sizes and colours described beautiful curved flights in the air and rained down amongst the delighted people. It did our hearts good to see how pleased they were – they were all of the poor peasant class – the bungalow next to ours followed our example, the crowd of recipients grew larger and got more excited – blowing us kisses, waving and demonstrating their thanks in every conceivable way. They quarrelled amongst themselves, and to our delight one man, who, thanks to his size and weight was getting more than his share, received a terrific box on the ear from an enraged woman and promptly departed. In case the reader should suppose that as prisoners of war, we had far too much food, I had better point out that much of this food was destined for future issues to individuals – several weeks' supplies were given away.

The rest of the camp now brought what surplus food they had not burnt and the fun continued. We were like schoolboys and threw many of our gifts to those who took our fancy. "There's a pretty girl!" Over goes a chocolate bar to her which she grabs and, smiles her thanks. "Look at that poor old chap; here you are Grandpa." Grandpa displays unexpected agility and seizes a well-aimed tin of salmon. Our only fear was that we should hit one of the over eager crowd who in the excitement of collecting food ignored the missiles that kept whizzing over. A tin of Klim thrown rather too low hit the telephone wires above the wall; the lid came off and a cloud of Milk Powder descended on the scavengers amid screams of laughter all round. Then a woman was hit by an English cheese tin and we feared she must be hurt badly as she was bleeding profusely from the face; however she seemed to recover but her friends would not take warning from her accident and a child was hit and knocked out. His father (evidently) merely carried him out of the way and continued to collect food. At last the Germans came along and tried to stop us, we ignored them; they drew their revolvers, we stopped throwing and the bungalow behind them started again; they turned to the other bungalow and we started throwing once more. More Germans arrived and the fun ceased. Two German sentries appeared amongst the crowd of Italians and slowly dispersed them. The girls made faces at them and pulled long noses at them behind their backs. One woman stopped to collect one more time, the sentry threatened her with his revolver; her child was screaming in terror; but ignoring the threat she seized the tin before moving away. We cheered her for her pluck, the revolver was turned on us – "Go on shoot, shoot defenceless men", shouted one chap in German, knowing full well that he would not do anything of the sort. The sentry scowled and moved on.

Later the S.B.O. informed us that the Germans had given orders that no food was to be burnt or thrown to civilians – we laughed, the good work had already been done. And there was no doubt now that anyone who escaped would be aided by the Italians.

We packed our kit and food for the journey, many people had Italian suitcases purchased through the canteen; but the majority of us were not so lucky and used pillow cases, sheets or blankets etc. in which to carry our kit.

I decided to hide and let the party go without me, but discovered that about 200 other people had the same idea. Under the theatre stage, in a huge pile of wood for the kitchens, in the water cisterns, in the roof; in fact in every conceivable place that could hide a man there I found others. One chap turned on the water in the ablutions room – "stop it you ass", came an anguished cry; the startled searcher for water looked round in astonishment and saw a head appear from the cistern, formerly dry, but now rapidly filling with water. In one bungalow the occupants were a little surprised but highly amused when one of His Majesty's officers suddenly descended into their midst accompanied by a shower of dust, lathes and plaster. One of the "roof hiders" had been a little careless. There were many other equally funny incidents too numerous to mention. Spirited optimists commenced digging holes in which to hide; one super optimist was standing between two double doors locked on the inside. After enduring cramp with commendable fortitude for several hours, he came to the brilliant conclusion that he could not keep it up for several days and so desisted. In the end most of the "Hide up Brigade" gave up the attempt. One or two remained (viz in a tunnel that had been started many weeks previously) and some of these did thereby escape including those chaps in the tunnel. That night the Germans kept a more vigilant eye on us and so far as I know, nobody got away that night.

—

This diary has assumed larger proportions than I had anticipated. It is I fear badly written and expressed. But should you wish for more; there is another book to come; which through practice will, I hope, make easier and better reading.

Book 2: Moosburg, Fort Bismark, Weinsberg

INTRODUCTION BOOK 2

It is now 21 April 1944 [Diary date - being written]

My diary has progressed very slowly. I am constantly forgetting to put various incidents in which are of general interest, and inserting details which can only be of interest to myself.

In apologising for the scrappy, poorly written and badly expressed Book 1, I must, in self defence, say that it was all written in a small room in which there were 11 other occupants and though we all like to be quiet at times, each of us has different opinions as to when that period of quiet shall be; with the inevitable result that we are always noisy.

Furthermore while deeply immersed in things of the past, I am constantly interrupted by things of the present. Cries of "Roll call" or "Tea up" or "Q.M. wanted" (such as my role at present) and similar interruptions make an already woolly and overcrowded memory seethe with confusion, and cause a scratching and wavering pen to become almost unmanageable; and an uncertain syntax is thereby swollen into a mass of subordinate clauses, split infinitives, adjectival phrases, such as might well cause all my past instructors to reel with horror. As for the crossings out –!?

However, I shall persevere and here goes –

12 SEPTEMBER 1943

At 3 a.m. in the morning we reluctantly left our beds and prepared for our journey. In semi darkness we assembled on the parade ground and were counted; then counted again; by about 4.30 we were all ready to move, and it was just getting light – in the true tradition of any army we had 3 hours to wait before we moved. We accordingly made ourselves comfortable, stools were brought out, a gramophone started playing and those officers who were not leaving that day provided tea.

It was a glorious morning and as P.O.Ws we had learnt to take things as they came. I strolled along the ranks to see how many of my friends were going. There were about 700 officers and a weird sight, they were dressed in all uniforms from tropic kit to greatcoats, an amazing variety of hats, caps and sun helmets, and an even stranger collection of suit cases, kit bags, blankets, sheets, string bags, valises, packs, haversacks (army pattern and home made, Italian, German and British).

At last we moved off in threes; amid shouts of goodbye, good luck and so [on] and so forth from those remaining behind. At the rear of this fantastic column moved two handcarts piled high with kit some of which was already falling off. Many officers were hopelessly overladen with kit and one fainted before we had moved 300 yards. I believe he was taken back to the camp hospital. As we proceeded towards the town of Modena more and more bundles of kit were dropped, some were picked up by the Italian civilians and never seen again, but many of them carried them to the station for us. Ted and I had our kit slung on a long pole which we carried on our shoulders, unfortunately the kit swung to and fro between us and we progressed in an ungainly crablike style. The ranks were soon hopelessly confused as officers kept stopping to rearrange their heavy and ungainly burdens. In Modena the streets were crowded with women and children but very few men. News of our generosity must have reached them for most of them gave every indication of liking us and loathing the Germans; at one time the crowd were intermingled with the prisoners, the harassed escorting sentries moved them back off the road, but not before at least two officers had managed to escape through the mass of civilians. One a short fellow was helped by an Italian girl who threw a shawl over his back just before a German sentry came up. The sentry thinking he was a girl (he could only see his back covered by a shawl – owing to the crowd) pushed him to one side with the rest of the civilians.

Ted and I sidled along with a tough looking German just behind us. At length we reached a level crossing; a large notice on the gates announced in both German and Italian that "saboteurs would be shot". We turned into the station and thankfully dropped our burdens and rested whilst waiting for our train. We were all drenched in sweat and somewhat weary and short of breath. Soon we all felt thirsty and turned to our water bottles for refreshment. There was some iron fencing alongside the station beyond which was a water tap; we persuaded some civilians on the far side of the fence to refill our water bottles, mine was broken as a result.[1]

Two more officers are said to have escaped here by jumping the fence at the crucial moment the German sentries were given cigarettes at that moment.

Eventually, we moved forward past a crude barrier at which we were counted; suddenly Ted said "Frank, your pillow case has fallen off the pole", I went back for it but alas it was gone, luckily it contained clothes and not food. Our train consisted of closed-in trucks – usually known as cattle trucks; they certainly smelt like it; some had obviously been used for coal. We were ordered into these trucks – 25 officers and their baggage per truck, they were hot, dirty, possessed no seating accommodation and no straw except that which had been left by the last occupants, which in our case we decided from the smell and litter must have been pigs. I found myself in a truck full of comparative strangers. However, they made me welcome, I squeezed in; the sliding doors clanged together and were bolted on the outside. There were 26 of us plus a large amount of kit, we could just lie down and that was all. Two small windows at each end of the truck let in a little light and air, were heavily guarded by barbed wire or iron grids.

It was now about 10.30 and getting extremely hot, we began to discard our scanty garments and sat naked but for a pair of underpants, yet the sweat was pouring off us. Already we felt thirsty and I began to regret the loss of my water bottle more and more.

We were shunted up and down the line and from our small windows we could see other trains of cattle trucks, all packed with prisoners, some English, many Italian soldiers and some civilians. Whenever a train of English prisoners passed us, there was a swift interchange of questions and answers. "Where from?" "Chieti and you?" "Modena and escapes?" "Quite a few – good luck" and away they would go. The Italian soldiers looked bewildered and fed up.

Time went on, our truck became yet more hot and stuffy and we all felt a little pessimistic, especially when we found that the German guard truck complete with mounted automatics etc. was immediately behind ours. Several trucks were opened and the occupants let out for a breather and purposes of nature. We had been in for about two hours and it was

---

[1]   We were warned to drink sparingly on the train owing to shortage of water.

a great relief to get out for a short while, but highly unpleasant returning to our foul abode.

I had a book "Selected English Short Stories" with which to pass the time, but was too interested in the conversation to read it. They were talking about the last few days and recounting stories of various attempts to hide, some of which I have already related. One more is worth mentioning i.e. that of an officer who hid himself in the enormous wood dump – 3 months supply for the kitchens. So well did he conceal himself that he found it impossible to get out. A major strolling past was startled when an anguished voice demanded his assistance in very forthright language. The major recovered himself and made a few fractious remarks about the folly of British officers playing at "house" in a pile of wood. The reply was so lurid that even the major was impressed and with the assistance of others released the escapee who had so effectively trapped himself.

13.00 hrs. At last the train started, and we discovered the inadequate swinging accommodation of cattle trucks. The truck bumped, jolted, rattled and bounced like an ancient Ford driving at speed over rocks. An exasperated voice enquired whether all the wheels were square instead of round. The jolting made it difficult to read and the windows were too high to be able to see anything unless one remained standing which was a highly difficult feat. We travelled due north and very fast which helped to cool us a little.

At about 5.30 we stopped at a place which most people think was MOLTAVA though heated arguments have been held on the name of it. We had been travelling for about four and a half hours, I was very thirsty, we asked for "Vassa" (water) but there was none to be had, they let us out, one truck at a time and some trucks, ours included, were given two cases of fresh apples – my word they were good, sweet, crisp and juicy. An old Italian woman brought us some water in a bucket, it tasted filthy and obviously contained sulphur salts but it was cool and wet.

Soon we got back into our truck and moved off, night came on, but it grew hotter rather than colder. By carefully stacking our baggage we managed to lie down flat; the water we had drunk made us sweat and we lay stark naked with the perspiration pouring out of us. The floor smelt worse than ever, we were filthily dirty and so exceedingly tired that we soon slept when it got dark. I woke up during the night about 2 a.m. I imagine. I was cool at last, in fact a little chilly. I put on a shirt and trousers and looked out of the window; I thought then we must have reached the Brenner Pass (actually we were still a long way from it), for we were going through splendid mountain scenery in the moonlight. I could see great rocks towering above us on our right, through the other window I could see little but occasional weirdly shaped hillocks and craggy hills silhouetted against a starry sky. We were travelling in a huge curve and I could see the engine far ahead of us, I do not know how many trucks there were in that train but it was extraordinarily long.

13 SEPTEMBER 1943

Soon after dawn we stopped at a small alpine village very much the picture postcard type – no one appears to know its name.

We were not allowed out at this pretty little place, though we remained there for nearly an hour. We stopped again some two hours later, and this time we were let out for purposes of nature, which purposes were relieved in full view of several women who seemed neither surprised nor shocked. Here the Germans discovered that several officers had escaped. Two had unscrewed a grating in their truck, climbed through on to the buffers and as the train slowed down, jumped off. Both these officers are known to have reached Switzerland. One truck load of officers smashed a hole through the floor; three officers then descended through the hole while the train was stationary, they lay down flat between the rails and the train moved off. The sentries on our train did not spot them but unfortunately another trainload of prisoners arrived as ours departed. The sentries on this train saw them, recaptured them and handed them over to our guards at the next station.

Our train was under command of a German R.S.M. of the worst type. He was furious with the three officers and ordered them to be bound with thin wire, this was done and they were put on the Guard's carriage in the sun which was by now very hot, there they were to remain for two hours. At the end of two hours they were released from their agony by a German sentry; who was severely punished by the R.S.M. for doing so without permission, notwithstanding the fact that the 2 hours had elapsed.

At about midday we reached LAVIS, evidently a small village at the foot of the mountains. By this time we were unspeakably dirty, unshaven and parched with thirst. Several South Africans said it was worse than being in a tank in the desert. But here we were let out, one truck at a time and escorted out of the station for about 50 yards to a steep hill. On the left at the side of the road was a ditch about 2 feet deep and wide; down it flowed ice-cold, crystal-clear water at a tremendous pace (obviously a minute mountain stream) [and] in full view of several women and children we stripped stark naked and washed ourselves, one could just lie down in that narrow stream, and after our filthy hot carriage it was the most invigorating and delightful bathe I have ever had. Though they kept urging us to hurry, I just managed to have a quick shave. There was an old brewery yard by our washing place where we refilled our water bottles. As we left to return to the train I saw the three officers referred to, in the last page, being escorted for a wash. Their waists and hands were swollen and their faces bruised, they looked pretty "done in". In order to reach the station we had to pass a small café or hotel; as we did so the German R.S.M. appeared and summoned one of our escorting sentries with a loud bellow. The sentry ran up to him and stood rigidly to attention, he received a smart slap in the face and a storm of furious language. The other sentry grinned to us "The R.S.M. has been drinking and is angry", he said in German. Apparently the unfortunate sentry was being soundly [be]rated for allowing us so long to wash. Like all the guards he was very young, barely 21. Refreshed and invigorated we returned to our home in the Cattle Truck. The mortified sentry urging us to hurry and venting his anger at the R.S.M.'s treatment of him, tried to hasten our climbing into the truck by punching and hitting our rear regions, in our efforts to obey his orders he was unfortunately kicked in the chest. He did not know who was responsible and so muttering angrily he shut us in. My long legs had avenged a slightly bruised posterior. Before the train left our interpreter came down the line and told us not to escape unless we were certain of success. He was in the same carriage as the S.B.O., Adjutant and the German R.S.M. On the S.B.O.'s behalf he had frequently requested the R.S.M. to let us out once every 2 hours (according to the Geneva Convention) and to ensure that all trucks were opened (one lot of officers were locked in for over 20 hours). The R.S.M. had replied that they were only Hottentots and was so furious when he discovered that many had escaped, that he vowed he would shoot anyone he caught trying to do so.

Once more we moved off and one fellow tried to make a hammock with a blanket; as slapstick humour it was a complete success. The Germans had discovered the hole in the truck which I have already mentioned, and all the remaining occupants had been squeezed into an already occupied truck making a total of 50 officers and their kit in one truck – poor devils. We also discovered that in their search of the train the Germans had helped themselves to our supplies of food and cigarettes. 50 of mine were missing and I was comparatively lucky. It was indeed lucky that we carried as much Red Cross food as possible, for except for the apples, and they were not given to everyone, we were given nothing.

We left LAVIS at about 3.30 pm. and in the evening reached BOLZANO which had obviously [been] bombed recently. We could see one railway bridge that must have received a direct hit. We stopped here for several hours and were asleep before we left. We were not allowed out at all nor could we get any water. The station was a big one and crowded with people. But they all looked disillusioned and far from cheerful – very different from an English station. The people were defeated and took little interest in us. That night we passed through the Brenner Pass and stopped at Innsbruck the next morning 14 September at about 8 am.

14 SEPTEMBER 1943

Thus we had been locked in for about 17 hours or more and were once again grimy and dishevelled. Here we again had an opportunity to wash in another but much larger mountain stream; this one was far from clean and was so fast flowing that we were not allowed to get in it, but washed as best we could squatting on the edge. This time our escort was a 'last war' veteran who though he tried to hurry us, was preferable to the bumptious youngster of the day before.

Innsbruck is a large station, it was full of trains laden with P.O.Ws and soldiers. Our lavatory was a little more decent than before (a large hole and a screen of sacking) but hopelessly inadequate for the number of prisoners who wished to use it.

We returned to our truck and were told to treat German officers with respect. Two of our own officers had their hands in their pockets while a German officer was counting us, they removed them and the affronted German continued his counting.

Soon we moved off again and passing through Munich (little bomb damage could be seen) we arrived eventually at Moosburg. Where to our joy we finally quit our cattle trucks and marched to a P.O.W. camp about half a mile from the station. When we reached the camp which was a very large one we stopped just inside the wire and received cups of water from the Free French Officer prisoners – we were all delighted, the German interpreter advised us not to drink too much cold water on an empty stomach but we were too thirsty to worry about the consequences and drunk and gargled the delicious liquid until we were ordered to move on.

We marched through the camp to our own compound and passed prisoners of all nationalities, Russians, Poles, Czechs, Greeks, French and Belgians. Each compound being wired with barbed wire about 10 foot high, with walks between for sentries. Search lights and machine guns were mounted at the necessary places and large Alsatians were led about on a chain by German sentries on patrol. Our living quarters consisted of several bungalow huts containing treble rack wooden beds in groups of 4, which reeked of insecticide and the palliasses were filled with straw, wood shavings and louse powder. They had obviously been used by many P.O.Ws before us. I slept on the top bunk where my head was about 1 foot from the roof. There were tables and forms for our meals and no space to spare anywhere. But after our cattle trucks, it seemed delightful. We slung our kit on to our beds, were issued with an old blanket each and went outside to investigate. Apart from our own and other similar bungalows there was only one other building, namely a latrine and wash house; in which most of the wash basins were broken; and in which the most sanitary arrangement was a liberal supply of chloride of lime.[2]

We cleaned up our bungalow as best we could and received our rations, potatoes, margarine, bread and some sort of stew. Then the bugle blew, we formed up in fives and were counted, recounted and counted again. Finally, the Camp Commandant arrived with his interpreter. The Commandant was a stout old chap, obviously he had served in the last War, and he proceeded to give us a long address in German, stopping after each sentence while his interpreter translated for us into a form of English which was nearly as unintelligible as its German equivalent.

In brief, what he said at very great length was this, that the Herr Hauptman (Captain) Commandant welcomed us to Moosburg. Where if we behaved well he would treat us well. Nevertheless, it was an Officers camp and we would soon be moved to a better camp. He then told us that it was forbidden to carry fire arms, insult sentries and so on and so forth. Finally, he insisted on us paying compliments to German officers, directed our attention to the Geneva Conventions posted in the camp, told us the times of meals, roll calls etc. and then departed, none too soon for we were on the verge of laughter. He was a courteous old chap in spite of his volubility and told one of our German-speaking officers that he had instructed Rommel as a cadet.

A French orderly assisted us in keeping our bungalows clean etc. When we returned from the Commandant's address I found him talking to a short tubby little man dressed in shabby serge trousers and a coat

---

[2]   In each bungalow there was also a small washroom with one tap and a pump. "To have a bath" meant to strip naked and crouch under the pump till clean.

rather too large for him. This little man grinned at me, "Me Rusci!" he said. "Il est Russe", said the French orderly. I gave him a cigarette and some food, he grinned again and left our hut. How he had got out of the Russian compound and into ours I do not know, but we discovered later that he was famous for his prowess in crossing the highest and thickest barbed wire fences in the camp. He spent most of his time in visiting the compounds of other nationalities and "acquiring" food. Ever since then we always spoke of the Ruscis in preference to the Russian. After he had left, I found that my B.D. [Battle Dress] blouse had also left. On one side of our compound were some Czechoslovakian Officers and a few Greeks. On the other side there were French Officers and O.Rs, also some Poles. Beyond one end of our compound the Russian O.Rs lived, with our own O.Rs adjoining, though wired off.

We strolled round our area trying to talk to our various allies, swapped cigarettes etc. through the wire and exchanged news. Our linguists had the time of their lives. Though it soon got dark, the camp was lit up by the lights on the barbed wire, and the innumerable search lights which probed and swept every corner of the camp. The Russian compound were very cheerful, they sang and danced to the strains of a dilapidated violin; our men then burst into some song and were loudly applauded; the French then made a few vocal efforts and so it went on until 10.30 when we had to return to and remain in our bungalows.

The Camp interpreter lost no time in pumping us with a little anti-Russian propaganda. We were advised to keep watch all night in case they came in to our compound and stole our kit; on being asked how the Russians could cross the wire, lit up as it was, in view of the sentries, the interpreter merely shrugged his shoulders.

15 SEPTEMBER 1943

The next day, 15 September after morning roll call, we had another look round; in the door of each hut was a list of punishments awarded to previous offenders. Most of them were for offences against German women (willing or unwilling) for which the award was a maximum of 3 years. The opportunities for such misconduct arose when prisoners were on working parties, in which case they were very inadequately guarded, often when working on farms etc. they would live on the farm itself, right away from the camp, with very few guards; the German women were mostly very forward, and hence the trouble. It can well be imagined that such a state of affairs favoured attempts at escape, of which there were many, but few were successful, because there was little food to be had, the Swiss frontier was extremely well guarded and comparatively few of the prisoners on working parties could speak German.

Probably owing to the Germans there were many stories about the Russian P.O.Ws. I include two of them here without in any way claiming them to be true.

One morning the Ruscis refused to come out of their bungalow to parade for roll call; the Germans sent an Alsatian in to drive them out, these dogs are specially trained and very strong and fierce against P.O.Ws (they snarl and snap at one, if one passes near them). Having sent their dog in, the Germans waited for results; nothing happened, finally a Rusci popped his head out of the door and asked them to send in another dog. On entering themselves, the German discovered their dog, he had been killed and skinned, and was now simmering on the fire. The Russians said they would still be hungry after eating him, hence their desire for another. This story caused riotous amusement and contrary to German designs, raised them in our estimation.

The second story was, that [when] one Russian died, his comrades hid his body under the floor, and continued to draw his rations until the body was discovered. The idea of swindling the Germans for more food than they were entitled to get, however gruesomely obtained, again appealed to us.

Lastly in some inexplicable way the Russians always had knives on them; which of course is strictly forbidden, they were constantly searched and their knives confiscated and were not even allowed the nearly harmless domestic knife with which to eat their food; yet they invariably obtained more, the source of which the exasperated Germans could never discover.

The amount of bribery and corruption of the guards that was carried on at Moosburg was unbelievable, especially because few of the P.O.Ws received Red Cross parcels, though some of them including the Serbs occasionally received some from the American Red Cross. One could always ascertain the latest news as per Alvar Lidell, several P.O.Ws are said to have left the camp for a day or two and returned at their leisure, with any article or game that they had pinched or poached. How much of this and other stories is true one cannot tell, but the Russians undoubtedly had knives and there was undoubtedly an intimate acquaintance with Joseph MacCloud.[3]

We ourselves did little but listen to these stories and laugh at the way the Russians deceived and made fun of the Germans. One German officer rode down to the Russian compound, lent his bicycle against a hut and went inside; while he was there one Russian promptly ripped both tyres with a knife, grinned at us and vanished before the officer returned. When the officer did return, he started with surprise, shook his fist at the man[y] P.O.Ws who were laughing at him and wheeled away his battered bicycle.

We spent several happy [h]ours watching some Russians erect a barbed wire fence, between our own compound and the road leading to the main entrance of the camp. They were under the supervision of two German sentries and obviously did not intend to work hard for Germany, also we made an appreciative audience. Never have I known men work so slowly; very carefully with much time and trouble the post would be inserted in a hole in the ground and firmed up. The barbed wire was then nailed on; when the sentry was not looking, they would pull out the nails, and snip the barbs off the wire; then one of them would poke the dog in the ribs, and dart out of his reach, the animal would leap at the offender snarling and growling, and nearly pull the sentry to which he was chained, right off his feet.

We had one issue of Red Cross parcels at Moosburg; besides the food we carried personally, one truck load of parcels had also been brought with us. The rest of the camp all wanted tea, the German ersatz equivalent tastes vile, and we were getting short of "fags", hence much business was conducted through the wire and after much bargaining most of us obtained prices varying from 20–25 cigarettes for a packet of tea.

The Adjutant gave each room a talk on our position and amongst other things, told us that the Commandant at Modena had escaped with about ½ million lira of cash. The money held in the camp as backing for the token money we received for our pay. Many of our Italian Officers at Modena were now themselves supposed to be prisoners of the Germans. Prisoners from Bologna camp also brought interesting information. There the Italians told the Germans that the P.O.Ws were armed; actually they were not, they had however made several gaps in the wire. A large party of them walked out of the camp and were fired on by some Germans; the

---

[3]   Alvar Lidell and Joseph MacCloud were both newsreaders on BBC Radio.

German officer apologised afterwards saying that he understood that they were armed. Meanwhile the Germans had brought up a couple of tanks whose guns covered the camp and a platoon of Infantry put in a very orthodox attack. As one P.O.W. said, "It looked like a demonstration of 'fire and movement'." So far as I know, no one was hurt, and again the Germans apologised and said that the Italians had told them that the camp was armed with Italian rifles and automatics.

We received a letter card and a postcard each, together with minute instructions as to how they were to be written, folded etc.; and what we were not allowed to write and so on. I wrote to home and to 'Mary'[4]; my letter home definitely reached its destination after about 6 weeks; the Germans told us it would take from 10–21 days. The Americans gave us 10,000 marks, for some clothing and with this we bought several barrels of German beer, which was quite good.

We only stayed at Moosburg for 6 days and spent most of that time in "yarning" amongst ourselves and to our neighbours, playing bridge, patience, and other card games and watching the various incidents which occurred almost hourly in the Camp. In a very short time "Stoofas" and various homemade cooking contrivances sent their reeking fumes up towards heaven, as the inevitable cups of tea were "brewed". My efforts in this direction were a successful failure. After an hour of collecting fuel, forming a stove of large stones, retrieving cardboard and other fuel blown away by the wind, lighting and relighting my fire, coaxing, blowing and cursing it, I at last obtained some very smoky water which was slightly discoloured by dust and tea. Proudly I bore it into my bungalow and promptly dropped it on colliding with someone; sadly I surveyed the result of my handiwork as it spread over the floor forming little balls of dust laden water. The same one who was partly responsible turned out to be a gentleman of the highest order; for after only ten minutes he brought me a cup of steaming hot tea. I thanked him and asked him how he had achieved such a miracle in such a short time; "The French orderly did it for me", he said. "Too easy", he smiled maliciously.

Three days after our arrival, there was a great stir in the camp; on going out to discover the cause, we saw a large party of important looking gentlemen walking down the main road in the camp. They were very senior officers of the Italian Army and some eminent looking civilians. Rumours swiftly spread. They were part of the Italian embassy, they

---

4   Mary Dee, Frank's fiancée whom he married on 30th April 1946.

were the Italian Army representatives in Germany; various other ideas were published but it was generally considered from such information as we could obtain from the Germans that they were in fact part of the Italian Embassy. In any case they were now prisoners and our mirth was somewhat malicious.

19 SEPTEMBER 1943

On 19th September we were told to be ready to move on the morrow, at 2.30 A.M. (groans). We divided ourselves into parties of friends and packed our kit; I had little left to pack. There were the usual rumours as to our destination; and STRASBOURG became a hot favourite and, strange to say, we did in fact go there. That evening the Russians and our own other ranks sang more than ever. The Russians sang the Red Army songs and other songs obviously of a patriotic nature, our fellows kept singing sentimental slush, "The White Cliffs of Dover" etc. but were heartily applauded by the Russians who obviously thought they were English patriotic songs.

20 SEPTEMBER 1943

On 20th September at 2.00 A.M. a sleepy and disgruntled lot of officers clambered out of their bunks and made tea with hot water provided by the kitchens, ate a small breakfast, and stumbled out into the darkness, through the gate in the barbed wire and formed up in their respective parties. Of course a few of them could not find their parties and there was a lot of shouting. "What number party are you[?]" Some humourist would then tell them the wrong number so that it was some time before the whole parade was in order. During this time, searchlights and torches flashed and darted around us and German sentries encircled us. We were ready to move by about 2.30 but evidently the German Wehrmacht was not and it was not until 4 o'clock that we moved, when we marched for 200 yards and stopped. It was now slowly getting light, and rain began to fall slowly and wettingly. We soon realised the reason for the delay – another search. We moved another 100 yds and stopped again and so it went on. Once our group stopped outside the camp gaol. Two Americans peered through the heavily barred windows, they had been imprisoned for attempting to escape, one of them (so I was told) had plenty of German money and had travelled many miles by train before being caught. At last my party were searched, by this time as was always the case, the searchers were tired and did not do their job at all thoroughly. As soon as we had been searched, we passed through the main gate where we were each given a loaf of bread and a slice of German sausage which smelt too strongly of garlic and looked too naked to be appetising. However it was an agreeable surprise that we got anything at all. We were marched down to the station where, contrary to an optimistic rumour of 3rd class carriages, we found the usual cattle trucks awaiting us on a siding. This time 40 of us had to get into each truck, but as the weather was much cooler and as our truck contained forms we managed to sit down in comparative comfort though we were so tightly packed, that to eat any food was a work of art. Profiting by my previous experiences I had obtained a beer bottle from the French orderly and filled same with water for the journey.

No sooner had our party settled down in our truck than the rain which previously had been a fitful drizzle, now come down in earnest. We watched the remainder of the P.O.Ws standing in the rain waiting for their trucks to be shunted on to the siding. Many a witty remark was made by those already in the train to those standing outside. It so happened that all the senior officers and those who were in any way unfit through wounds or ill health were in a separate group as they were going to another camp, and it was these unfortunate fellows who were now standing in the rain.[5] However they all took it in good part, and had the laugh on us later on. At last they too got into their trucks, but we did not move off for another hour or so.

In fact our timetable was as follows: Reveillé 0200, Formed up 0250, Moved 0400 (searched for 2 minutes each), Entrained 0900, Train moved 11.45. Thus we had had 9 hours doing little else but standing and waiting. The journey lasted about 20 hours and was in every way better than the previous one. The weather was much cooler, it rained most of the time, and though we were more crowded, the forms enabled us to make the best use of the space; in addition the sentries sat in the same trucks as ourselves and for most of the journey, the doors were open. Lastly we had articles in each truck for such relief as nature made inevitable. In one truck they made friends with the sentry who being very 'green' did not keep hold of his rifle, it was removed without him seeing it; and a naval officer made a gallant leap for freedom, but the train was travelling too fast and he was badly hurt; he was spotted and picked up and returned

---

[5] Several of them had Italian suit cases which became saturated with rain and rapidly changed shape until they resembled a kit bag.

to us about 6 weeks later none the worse for his adventures except for the loss of one arm which had been amputated above the elbow; it was astonishing how quickly he recovered. (There now!! I have just been told that this attempt was made on our next journey and that the naval officer climbed through the hole left when he had removed the grating from the side of the truck.) In several trucks, ours included, we showed great interest in the sentry's rifle and succeeded in getting it out of his hands but the train travelled too fast for anyone to follow up the advantage, whenever we slackened speed the sentry took his rifle from us. I should have said that before leaving Moosburg we had to pack all our food in separate parcels, and they were all loaded on a single truck. We were only allowed to retain 2 tins of food for the journey. The reason for this was obvious, they hoped to limit our chances of escape by allowing us sufficient food for one day only; however the search was so inefficient that most of us managed to bring rather more. We reached AUGSBERG at about 5.30 pm. and here several officers got underneath their trucks for those purposes for which our trucks were not equipped, and were highly embarrassed when the train moved forward a little leaving them quite in the open. Modesty is an inconvenient virtue for a P.O.W.

Our next stop was outside MUNICH, we could see little of the town and were not allowed out of the train.[6] After we had moved off, we began to settle down for the night – a most difficult proceeding. We were tired of sitting on forms and most of us were complaining of cramp (excuses to obtain a little more room). In spite of my length, I manage, after some pushing, edging, moving of bundles of kit, apologising, grumbling to get stretched out at full length on the floor under one of the forms, to the great amusement of the rest of them. The relief to my aching legs was great; and gently but firmly I removed a pair of boots from my face and composed myself to sleep. A sharp dig in the ribs, from a jumpy officer's boot was rather disconcerting but before long I fell asleep, to the lullaby of bumps, jerks, the rattle of wheels and an occasional snort from my companions.

---

[6]	I think it was at Munich that a German asked us in English where we had been captured. We replied CALAIS he looked surprised and a sentry shook his fist at us.

21 SEPTEMBER 1943

On 21st September we awoke, stiff, sore, cramped, unshaven, dirty and generally dishevelled, however this was nothing new. There were the usual remarks about what we would like for breakfast and how hot we would like our baths etc. as we munched our garlic flavoured German sausages and such food as we had each brought with us. At about 7.30 we arrived as STRASBOURG and here slowly, truck by truck we all left the train for good except the "old folks" previously mentioned; it was still raining a little and the senior officers from the shelter of their cattle trucks bid us farewell and wished us luck. We were sorry to see them go, many of us had lost personal friends and Eric Lestrange had to part from his Father, Colonel Lestrange; he could have accompanied him had he wished to do so but thought he would have been a little out of place in a senior officers' camp. Here too Colonel Shuttleworth our S.B.O. left us. Whilst bidding us goodbye from their trucks, the "Old Folks" made many facetious remarks about the weather, the snugness of their carriage and so on. At last we moved away from the siding to the shelter of the goods yard store and settled down to the usual wait. A German C.S.M. [Company Sergeant Major] was 'throwing his weight about' shouting orders to his men and darting about the station for no apparent reason. We tried to talk to some porters who were lolling about watching us. Now Strasbourg is in Alsace-Lorrain[e] and we hoped the inhabitants might be friendly. The porters however said little and eyed our sentries. One of them remarked that they did not know their nationality because it changed so frequently; at the moment they were Germans and had to behave as such. Meanwhile our parcels of food had been dumped in the yard and loaded in a truck by several of our other ranks, they were driven off to the camp and after some time, returned for more. "What is it like?" we asked. "Shockin' place Sir, looks like an old fort, no one else there; we did not see very much of it but it looked very dismal." Inspired by this cheering news we morosely turned our attention to the goods yard again. There were very few people about and the porters had disappeared.

At last we moved out of the station and were as usual counted and recounted and then to our astonishment we were told that we were travelling by tram. The trams when we saw them, were small and possessed one compartment only (no upper floors for the smokers). There were about 20 of them joined together in a continuous train. We boarded them and by carefully imitating the sardine, managed to get the required number in each compartment. A sentry stood on the footboard of each tram and having been warned to cause no damage, we started off. In our tram was a civilian conductor, a French boy he cannot have been more then 15 years old and looked less. Between the sentry and ourselves was a closed door, and the French boy talked freely. Though young, he was intelligent and was obviously speaking the truth. He told us that as a whole the inhabitants of Strasbourg and indeed most of Alsace-Lorraine were pro-British, most of them very strongly so and that all of them loathed the Germans. They were short of food and very short of tobacco and cigarettes; so were we but we took the hint and he put the cigarettes given to him into his pocket and thanked us. He then continued, they were short of cigarettes yes, and so were the Germans. Clothing was very hard to obtain, especially boots and shoes. My French is not good and much of his conversation I could not understand, but I was seated near an obliging linguist who told me the above. He then told several stories of various incidents in which the Germans had behaved abominably and in which the French had retaliated as best they could. He told us the Swiss border was very well guarded, which we knew, and did not advise us to escape unless we had plenty of food because the people had barely enough to live on themselves and would probably be too frightened of the Germans to give us shelter. All this time we were travelling through Strasbourg, there were few people about, but some gave us the V sign. Many shops were shut, all appeared to be devoid of any goods whatsoever.

There were many German soldiers and officials and Alsatians in uniform; eventually we left the town and finally stopped, got out of our trams, bid adieu to our new young friend to whom we had given all the news we had heard, much of which he did not know, and formed up in the road and were counted. It was still raining as we marched through a small building estate, in which the houses were modern but very attractive with their steeply sloping rooves and gables situated in small neat gardens. We could see into many of the houses, which looked snug and homely. Here an elderly woman was cooking, there an old man was tending his garden in spite of the rain, dusters were shaken out of windows and all the domestic tasks were being done just as at home. All of us were, I think reminded of our own homes by these simple sights. Then I heard a gasp of admiration; and saw a radiant vision of loveliness staring at us (we must have looked like a collection of tramps); she was very fair, slim and very pretty, she gave us a quick smile and disappeared inside a house. We carried on towards our prison, our lot made more dismal by comparison. In fact it was a damp and dejected lot of officers that halted outside the barbed wire of Fort BISMARK as it was now called, the previous name had been obliterated and was illegible; the new name was on a board over the doorway. We stared down, on to the fort; down, because the whole fort was built in a pit and its roof was level with the ground and covered with growing grass and trees; between us and the fort was a moat which was quite dry and about 50 feet wide, and about 12 feet deep at its shallowest. Across the moat was a large wooden bridge, large enough and strong enough for a small lorry to cross. This bridge led to the porch of the fort in which were two huge iron doors.

We entered the gate in the wire and were of course counted yet again, we crossed the bridge and entered our new home. It was dark, damp, smelt must[y] and unused and looked and felt cold and forbidding. After some time we separated into the various rooms and I eventually found myself in the same room as Mould, Edwards, Jack Wright and about 20 others. The three officers whose names I have given had been with me at Modena in our passage room; so I was with old friends.

In each room were two large racks, one above the other along the entire length of one wall; these were our beds, on them were clean palliasses filled with clean, dry bracken – luxury. We four were lucky in that we secured the top rack; dust and bits of bracken fell like rain on those sleeping below. The rest of the room contained two large tables and forms which were just sufficient for most of us to sit down together, a small stove and two electric lights completed our furniture but for a couple of long shelves. We were each issued with 2 sheets but no blankets, an enamel bowl, a small hand towel and a china basin for our food.

On exploring the fort we discovered that we were all confined to the back of it, the front (looking towards France) was walled off completely except for two iron doors which were locked, the key hole revealed little or nothing. There were two stories, the bottom or basement being on a level with the bottom of the dry moat and the top just below ground level. The fort was we discovered built in 1871, it had obviously not been occupied for some time, the ironwork was rusty, the whitewash peeled off the stone and concrete walls and such woodwork as there was (i.e. on which the electric wiring was fixed) was mostly rotten. The washing accommodation was poor, the water supply worse and it was only through hard work by our stalwart cooks that the kitchens sufficed to feed us. The only place which we had for exercise was the dry moat, in to or over which (according as whether you were in the basement or top floor) all our windows looked. This moat was almost, but not quite dead straight, and was about 200 yards long. At each end of the moat a machine gun was mounted commanding almost the whole moat; naturally these guns were always manned, they were on ground level and so had a bird's eye view of us in the moat. At the bottom of the moat at each end was a single strand of wire and just beyond it a tangled mass of barbed wire. An entirely unnecessary notice announced "Any P.O.W. attempting to cross this wire will be sharply shot." The machine gun added weight and meaning to this somewhat puzzling notice. The far side of the moat was supported by a brick wall about 10 feet in height, beyond which was a small bank with a barbed wire fence, not very thick, running along the top of it. On the bank and partly in the wire a thin screen of young rowan, ash and sycamore saplings were growing together with tall rough grass and brambles; in places the screen of growth was quite thick.

Two sentries walked up and down beyond the wire; however owing to the brambles etc. they could not see the barbed wire very clearly although it was only 3 or 4 yards from them.

Now I have said that the moat was nearly straight, but this rough sketch plan will make it clearer. *See* Figure 1: Sketch of Fort Bismark.

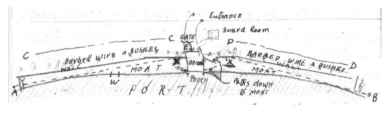

Sketch of Fort Bismark

A and B are the two machine guns mounted at either end and the dotted lines show how their lines of sight were limited by the curve of the Fort. Thus there was a blind spot X – X near the bridge which was not covered by either of the machine guns. The two sentries beyond the wire whose beats are shown as C – C and D – D could only see the wire in places owing to brambles and young saplings. The last sentry E stood by the gate and could see little beyond the bridge. Hence X was almost entirely out of view though sentry D might be able to see it through the young trees. We nearly all spotted this blind spot the first day and full use was made of it before the Germans themselves discovered it.

The rest of the day we spent in making ourselves as comfortable as possible and washing and shaving. Inside the fort the washroom was on the bottom floor and was hopelessly inadequate to hold us all. In addition, the water was only turned on for certain periods in the morning and evening. Hence we had to carry our bowls full of water along seemingly endless stone corridors poorly lit by electric light which frequently failed and was always turned off during air raids after dark.

The fort was in the charge of a German O.F.W. (i.e. similar to a British Sergeant) or "Feldwebel"; it was too big a responsibility for him as he discovered to his cost.

Soon after our arrival we had a roll call, the numbers counted must have been incorrect for they soon had another and yet another. On this last parade someone laughed at the German Sgt who flew into a rage, drew his revolver, screamed for a machine gun to [be] brought and gibbered with rage. Nothing came of it, the sentries held their rifles ready, the machine guns were traversed on their mountings, in short, force was displayed but not used. Later a German officer arrived to whom Colonel Grobbelar complained about the Sergeant's behaviour. The Sergeant apologised and was thenceforth known as 'Bismark Billy', of whom more anon. They now altered their method of counting us, we had to march up the path onto and over the Bridge (in ranks of 5) where we were counted as we marched past the sergeant and so into the fort. The idea being to guard against counting the same man twice. But thanks to some quick witted P.O.Ws I doubt if they ever knew our correct total number. Hence making it difficult for them to ascertain if anyone was missing. In order to continue this state of affairs a little guile was necessary. At least eleven officers escaped from Bismark in as many days, some got home to England, several reached Switzerland, and two were recaptured on the borders of France. In addition there was one creditable but unsuccessful attempt that I witnessed.

Most of the escapes were made through the wire at the blind spot X (on sketch). Sentry D was easily distracted by a Scotch officer playing on some bagpipes which he had brought from Italy. The escapees then lay up in the undergrowth not 5 yards from Sentry D and crawled away when darkness fell.

The wall at X was at least 12 feet high and the escapees had to climb up on to the shoulders of their friends in order to scale it, and then worm their way through the wire, while their friends as best they could, obliterated any marks of their progress. In spite of their efforts a large hole was easily visible in the wire from the moat. On one occasion one of the Alsatian Dogs with sentry D barked furiously and we thought the game was up. But the sentry was unsuspecting and the officers got away.

After each escape it was necessary to fake the total number on roll call. This was easily done. Any officers who were sick did not go on parade but were counted separately inside the fort by the Sgt, who then walked out onto the bridge and counted the parade as they marched past him. Now the sick were tended by our own M.O. and only he could tell if they were shamming. Thus after each escape, the necessary number of fit officers reported sick and were counted with the genuine cases. Immediately the Sergeant had counted them they raced downstairs and got through one of the bottom windows into the moat, joined the parade and were counted again. This window is marked W on the plan and was in full view of the sergeant on the bridge and several sentries (there were always large numbers of sentries present for each roll call), but they were all so intent on watching the parade that it was several days before they spotted it.

By this means each couple of escapees got at least 36 hours start, then the parade would not be faked and the Germans would find that they were 2 short. When this occurred we were all kept out of the moat and sentries and dogs searched the fort, from top to bottom. The S.B.O. and Adjutant were questioned and at long length told the Germans absolutely nothing at all. The German officer who was now in charge said "Well you must know all about it but I suppose I cannot expect you to give away your comrades", and laughed the matter off. But they were very puzzled when every few days, they discovered that 2 officers had disappeared. They bricked up several doorways inside the Fort, put on a sentry inside the porch by night and evidently called in the local Gestapo. Long nosed earnest looking gentlemen, some of whom were civilians, came and stared suspiciously at the fort, moat, wire and ourselves. They prodded the walls, uncovered the man holes and then cut down many of the young saplings, fortunately not the right ones. All this occurred after the third escape was discovered. Two days later, two officers less. Another grand search, more earnest looking gentlemen came to stare at us and our home. A few days later and 3 more officers had disappeared (these only had 12 hours start as the Germans spotted the fit but sick officers as they came out of the bottom window. Then all the remaining saplings were cut down, the grass was scythed, the barbed wire was thickened and X was no longer a blind spot; but it had served its purpose.

It will be obvious that our first 10 days at Bismark were fraught with excitement, interest and amusement, in fact the interested onlookers nearly gave the game away on several occasions. But the extra roll call parades that inevitably occurred when the Germans could not get their sums right became very tedious and even the antics of the exasperated Germans failed to amuse us towards the end; several officers used to bark at the Alsatian dogs when they were at work, not for mere childish amusement only, but to excite them and distract their attention from their job. The results of such counter-barking were however very pleasing, the unfortunate German holding the dog would be pulled nearly off his feet and they had considerable trouble in quieting the animal sufficiently for him to continue his work.

Meanwhile our living conditions were very poor; we slept on our racks crowded close together. I am a restless sleeper and Cliff Mould and Padre Knight who slept on either side of me complained bitterly. The racks sloped so much that one tended to slide towards the bottom. The water was insufficient, the whole place was damp and musty and there was little to do. Cigarettes were now very short and there was no prospect of getting any more. The Germans assured us we should not be there long and were astonished at the letter which the S.B.O. and Adjutant addressed to the Protecting Power complaining of the treatment and conditions to which we were subjected.

On several nights there were air raids. Then the lights would be switched out at the main, often many of us would be washing or seeing friends and so not in our own room; in pitch darkness we would feel our way along the passages and try to find our rooms. We would enter one and ask what number it was; you usually got several answers, only one of which was correct, in fact it was a work of art to get to one's own room. Often there were so many in the passages, that as each man held on to the fellow in front, long crocodiles were formed, which for some obscure reason always started to run, causing much noise, laughter and confusion. On one such night Padre Knight had failed to make his bed, he accordingly lit one of his Church candles and set to work. Immediately there was a loud hullabaloo from the sentry outside on the far side of the moat. "Licht Aus, Licht AUS, LICHT AUS", he bellowed. We were by no means the only offenders and Padre said calmly "I am sure he is shouting at another room"; a bullet ricocheting off our stone window sill with a crack! and a whine! proved that he must have been wrong. "Well, I've nearly finished", said Padre placidly tucking in his blanket, while the hullabaloo outside rose in a grand crescendo, "Just shield the light will you." Eric French however was sleeping near the window and had every reason to be perturbed, he requested that the d–n thing should be blown out. A second crack! and a whine gave Eric a large majority and the candle was blown out by about 6 officers at once. I was well inside the room away from the window and gave the harassed Eric and his neighbours some friendly advice which was not appreciated. Then we lay back and listened; first a droning which got louder and louder until there was a steady, continuous, dull roar of engines; the R.A.F. music went on and on and on – it must have been a thousand-bomber raid, and we would feel rather than hear the distant detonations which were at Munich, as we heard afterwards.

The next morning the Germans complained about our infringement of the blackout regulations and the S.B.O. assured them we would behave in future. Padre Knight remarked that the Germans were so excitable. Eric French requested him to confine his activities to spreading spiritual light only.

After the Germans had cut down all the saplings, there were no more escapes. But two attempts I must mention. We were allowed to bring our remaining Red Cross parcels from Moosburg; when the lorry arrived from the station loaded with these parcels, both gates were opened and left open. We all turned out to unload the lorry; one officer picked up a Red Cross parcel and walked straight out through both gates. This bold bluff actually worked, no one stopped him but he was caught soon afterwards.

Another attempt was made by two Officers as follows. A large lorry used to drive down into the moat daily, to drain the cesspools. These two concealed themselves between the driver's cabin and the large sewage tank and were driven out of the fort in style, they too were soon recaptured.

There is little more to tell about Fort BISMARK; the weather became colder and the mornings misty, the Germans issued us with a little coal and we used to cook our Red Cross food in our rooms, the German-issued food being cooked in the kitchens and carried to each room. Cigarettes were so scarce that several of us smoked the German ersatz tea which looks and tastes like a handful of litter picked up in a wood, being composed of bits of leaves, dried lichen and dust. Though we were issued with it, no one would drink the concoction derived from it, so we smoked it and wished we had not. If we had had more to do, it would not have been so bad but there were very few books, not enough room for games, and we grew tired of cards.

We were all pleased when we were told that we were to be moved to a permanent camp. And were told that as we had to march several miles, we must tie up and label such kit as we could not carry. I had very little kit left and we had all practically finished our Red Cross food.

8 OCTOBER 1943

On 8 October we packed all our kit and dumped it outside as ordered, then we were searched by the local gendarmerie and a few soldiers; they were laughably inefficient and the search was a farce. Several of the gendarmes were pro-Allied being local Alsatians and made no pretence of searching except when Germans were present. They then decided to search our parcels so they all had to be brought back from the dump and there was a delightful muddle, which caused "Bismark Billy" to have a short attack of the tantrums; after this pleasing interlude, things were straightened out [and] we were ordered to be ready at the usual impossibly early hour of 3 AM.

9 OCTOBER 1943

After the usual confusion the parade was formed up in the moat by about 3.30. It was cold and dark but luckily – dry. We were counted by about four different German N.C.Os [Non Commissioned Officers] and the vacant fort was searched in case anyone had hidden up. "They needn't worry, no one would want to stay in this hole", someone rather aptly remarked.[7] It was dawn when we finally marched out of the fort and we were all delighted to go. We all enjoyed that march in the early morning, it was about 5 miles and we travelled by lanes and byeways through quaint old fashioned country villages and through fields, farmed on the strip system and often worked by P.O.Ws who waved to us, most of them were French and often there was no guard visible.

In one village we halted by the local gaol from which an English voice hailed us with an American twang. He had recently been shot down and was waiting to be removed to a P.O.W. camp. He had just time to give us the latest news and to receive a few gifts before we moved on. Along the country lanes grew numerous pear trees, laden with fruit, they were very juicy but sour. In throwing one away, someone hit one of our escort, who appeared to resent it considerably but failed to locate the culprit. After about 2½ hours we reached a long bridge over some marshalling yards, containing literally hundreds of sidings. What a target for the R.A.F!

---

[7] Nov 16 - 1944 – Have heard today of an officer who remained hidden at Bismark – now in England. He hid in a hole in the wall which was bricked up when he was in by his friends.

They have bombed in that area frequently since then, and must surely have dealt with this maze of railway lines.

There appeared to be no 'station' in the true sense of the word, and we turned off the road at the end of the bridge, and marched across a meadow towards the railway line; in this meadow we were again searched and again most of the searchers were local civilians who took little interest in their work. At last we reached the railway line on which a train of cattle trucks awaited us in a siding. The number of officers was again increased, this time there were 45 of us in each truck. The journey was however of short duration and the effects of crowding though unpleasant were not serious. We crossed the Rhine and stopped at HEILBRONN for some time where we watched the people in the station. There were many of them and all looked depressed, a wounded German soldier from the Russian Front grinned at us, there were several soldiers, ex AFRIKA CORPS, who showed great interest in us but the civilians mostly ignored us. Several plain clothes Gestapo were looking for someone in the crowd, the people obviously hated them, several girls grimaced at them when their backs were turned. Finally we reached WEINSBERG a pretty little country town (scarcely more than a village) about 5 miles from HEILBRONN situated in a fertile valley containing many small but steep hills.

Just outside the town was a conical shaped hill with the ruins of a castle or "schloss" on the peak. We arrived at about 5.30 p.m. disembarked and were formed up, counted again and again and after some little delay we moved off. We stopped just outside the station at a level crossing; some Russian P.O.Ws were unloading a truck of coal in a siding nearby, they smiled at us and one of them, by skilful use of his shovel, spilt coal dust over a German sentry near the track.

Most of the inhabitants, especially the children came to look at us but did not appear to be very hostile. The camp was barely quarter of a mile from the station and we soon passed through the inevitable barbed wire fences and gates into OFLAG VA [Offizierslager (a POW camp for officers); VA denotes the German military district] where most of us have remained until today, 5 May 1944, and look like remaining for several months to come.

When we arrived the camp was empty, obviously we were to start a new camp which is always trying, and we were sorry not to meet some other P.O.Ws. The camp inside the barbed wire consists in the main of two rows of hutted bungalows each about 50 yards long and 15 yards wide. The two rows are separated by the parade and sports ground of rammed ashes and stones, about 35 yards wide (between the bungalows) and about 500 yards long. Though wider in places.

24 SEPTEMBER 1944

Note: It is now 24th September 1944 and since the above was written our bungalows have been searched many times, and this diary has had to remain hidden; now it looks as though we shall be left alone for some time, hence it appears safe to continue. Unfortunately such a lapse of time is an additional burden to an already unreliable memory and the recording of exact dates becomes impossible.

TO RESUME:–

We marched on to the Parade Ground and were given a long harangue, similar to that [which] we had received on our arrival at Moosburg, telling us a few things that we must do, including the paying of compliments to German officers of senior rank to that of our own, and a great many things that we must not do; they persisted in the delusion that we had knives, pistols, guns and even heavier weapons of war concealed on our persons. It was nearly dark and getting decidedly chilly when selected officers "took over" the bungalows i.e. signed for every article of "furniture" and for "domestic" use in each room of every bungalow. Meanwhile we were paraded in groups, counted, checked and recounted and finally entered out new "home". Most of my friends and I found ourselves in Bungalow 25 and in Room number 5 of this Bungalow we proceeded to settle down.

(Cliff Moulds – Lincolns [The Lincolnshire Regiment]. Brian Lasc, Tom Weightman, Mike Davies – all D.L.I. Taffy Edwards and Rob Nixon – Royal Engineers. 'Lucky' Young – Midlothian [Midlothian Artillery Volunteers]. Ted Edwards – 1 Div Recce [1st Infantry Division Reconnaissance]. Ray Lever, Richard Garrett and myself – The Foresters. Nimmo-Smith. – N.H. Derek Lane – R.A. Finally Findlayson – R.A.A.F. [Royal Australian Air Force])

Fourteen of us altogether in a room about 15 feet x 24 feet together with seven double-bunks and about 7 cupboards 14 stools and two tables. There was really very little room, so little that to sit down at one of the tables was often a very difficult operation. However the room was clean and each of us had a china bowl, knife, fork, spoon and an aluminium mug. We went to bed firmly resolved to obtain more space in our room by fair or foul means and so ended our travels for many months.

10 OCTOBER 1943

There was plenty to do but little to eat. For breakfast we received a hot cup of tea – German ersatz, it tasted abominable but we had none of our own. We spent the morning in looking round the camp and realising how much would have to be done before we could be as comfortable and well organised as at Modena. At each end of the camp were deep "revetted" slit trenches the spoil from which was growing a few marigolds, nasturtiums and even fewer lettuces, onions and tomatoes.

Beside the dozen living bungalows two more pretentious buildings faced each other at the centre of the camp across the parade ground at its widest. These buildings were the kitchens and dining halls and contained sufficient forms and tables to feed the camp in two sittings, our strength was roughly 1100. By lunch time we were all very hungry, after lunch we were still very hungry, cabbage soup and potatoes entirely failed to satisfy us.

11 OCTOBER 1943

Most of us had brought some food from Bismark but our baggage was still being searched, or rather awaiting search and meanwhile we had very little to eat, practically nothing to read and no writing materials. So that by October 11th having become acquainted with the camp there was very little to do. Being a Sunday the Padre organised several services and the Germans refused to search and let us have our parcels. So that we had little to do, little to eat and very little to smoke, the burning question now was, "When shall we get some Red Cross parcels?" The S.B.O. Colonel De Beers had already sent a wire to Geneva and a letter as well, so that all we could do was wait as patiently as possible.

The camp was well guarded, a machine gun was sited at each corner, sited along the wire, sentries patrolled along the wire and there were two high wooden towers which overlooked the whole camp, and contained a sentry with a machine gun by day; gun and sentry were dismounted by night, but in smaller wooden erections searchlights, sentries and machine guns kept a close watch by night. In addition, Alsatians were used on patrols both inside and outside the barbed wire.

We soon discovered that our successful escapologists at Fort Bismark had made us famous and the authorities of this camp were very anxious for fear that these escapes might continue at Weinsberg.

12 OCTOBER 1943

The Germans commenced to search our parcels and in the camp itself various committees, bodies, organisations and clubs were born. The cloak and dagger department as it came to be called dealt with all camp intelligence; besides organising and assisting escapes, they worked in secret and in spite of the jests levelled at them, were very efficient in warning us of forthcoming searches etc. The library also struggled into being; after much argument with the Germans a room was set aside for the library and we were asked to contribute all our available books. When it first opened, there were rows of empty shelves with a few bedraggled and mutilated books. Now thanks to the Red Cross and the Y.M.C.A. new shelves have been acquired and are laden with books; another room has been obtained for non-fiction books and educational reference books. Besides which there are numerous text books held by various societies.

The bank also started at about this time and commenced the laborious task of ascertaining the pay and balance of cash in hand of every individual officer. The Education Committee under the guidance of Macquarrie commenced work, and before long timetables of lectures were drawn up, rooms were allotted for lectures, and one bungalow was eventually emptied and the rooms used for the library, the bank, the chapel, the post office, the central advertising bureau, the theatrical carpenters (Make and Break) and lecture rooms. All this took a great deal of time and concessions from our hosts were obtained with great difficulty; there were many delays and many difficulties before these and other organisations attained their present efficiency. The messing committee had the thankless task of feeding us on inadequate and unappealing food until the Red Cross supplies arrived. Other societies were the law society, engineering, farming, medical, music, and several more. Practically all commenced during our first few days at the camp. The theatre and the entertainments committee did not get going until later; they had a long period of arguing with the Germans before the lower mess was allowed to be used as a theatre, whereupon they set to work and erected a stage from the Red Cross packing cases and gave us one play a week thereafter.

However to return to Monday October 12th. We then had little to do; the German news in English was given to us over the wireless in the upper 'mess building' on that and every subsequent afternoon; we were not very interested in "Lord Haw Haw's" remarks but we were very interested in the German communiqués, which though guarded, did enable us to follow the course of the war. 'The Central News Agency', a body of German speaking officers and expert cartographers, soon produced large maps of Italy and Russia to enable us to follow events and indulge in the "Arm chair strategy" so beloved by all Englishmen, even when there are no arm chairs. At our evening meal of cabbage soup or, worse still, sugar beet leaf soup, a representative of the C.N.A. read the daily communiqué to us for the benefit of those who could not or would not listen to the wireless.[8] The news in German was also relayed later in the afternoon, hence those who could speak German and write shorthand soon became members of the C.N.A. The communiqués in English and those in German seldom differed, but as we were frequently unable to hear the first, or worse still, merely heard Haw Haw's chit chat and no communiqué, it was very important to obtain the news in German as well. The wireless was of course controlled by the Germans who often forgot or refused to switch it on, or would tune in to the wrong station. Hence the C.N.A. had and still have an arduous task.

13 OCTOBER 1943

For the remainder of that week, time passed very slowly; by Oct 13 the S.B.O. published a notice saying that he had heard from Geneva and about 5000 parcels were on the way. By now, most of us had finished any solid food that we had brought with us and were exceedingly hungry.

The few onions, lettuces etc. that had existed by the slit trenches ceased to do so. Had we had more to do, one would not have minded so much, as it was it was extremely hard not to think about food; hence this announcement cheered us all up and there were many discussions as to when the parcels would arrive. Several of us including myself smoked German tea which gave us no pleasure beyond amusing others. The weather was fine but chilly. We spent much of our time listening to each other's experiences and I give the following stories as being the most amusing and interesting.

---

[8]   At this time the Russians were attacking in the area of Krivoi Rog and Nicopol.

At camp No. 78 – 'Salmana' in Italy, after much hard work a tunnel had been dug from a bungalow under a cart track [and] under the barbed wire and ended in some bushes. All was ready for an escape by night. But the day before 'Nemesis' appeared in the shape of a donkey drawing a cart full of laundry along the track inside the wire. The asinine 'Nemesis' felt the ground give beneath her and her astonished driver saw her sink into the ground. 'Nemesis' broke her leg but her pursuit had not been in vain. The tunnel was discovered, long weeks of patient work had only one result. The cells.

At another camp in Italy the 'Carabinieri' used to watch the P.O.Ws from a hill outside of and overlooking the entire camp. They used field glasses to aid their study of the P.O.Ws and obviously hoped to spot any tunnelling operations or other efforts to escape. In order that these earnest gentlemen should not be disappointed several large holes were dug in which tins, messages etc. were buried. The Carabinieri returned eagerly to the camp and excitedly began to dig in the same places, their efforts were rewarded by a few tins and messages encouraging them to continue digging, this they did although with considerably lessened zeal until finally they realised that they had been fooled, and made an undignified exit amidst loud cheers from the interested P.O.Ws.

At yet another camp in Italy a tunnel had been successfully bored under the barbed wire and was thought to end under a small garden beyond which was a nearby house. It was imperative to know just where the tunnel ended, as they wished to continue with it until they reached some bushes where they had decided to make the exit. In order to test this an officer took a thin stick with him and wormed his way through the tunnel, he then pushed the stick up through the soil. The onlookers were horrified to see a man come out of the house and start work on the garden and sent word to the officer below. But they were too late, the gardener gasped with astonishment as a thin stick appeared from the ground rose vertically to about 1 foot from the ground and proceeded to wave to and fro. Recovering himself the gardener seized the stick and pulled; but the officer below was one of the bull-dog breed and not realising what was happening pulled harder; the stick slid through the gardener's hand and disappeared into the ground. The gardener, having lived near the camp, realised the position and reported the matter and hence the tunnel was discovered.

In several camps in Italy and subsequently in Germany well-planned escapes were frustrated at the last moment before the attempt took place. It was suspected that our hosts had "stooges" (i.e. disguised P.O.Ws) in the camps and the Germans certainly used well-concealed microphones as we soon discovered at Weinsberg. Here the Germans had a special room for the S.B.Os orderly room; the S.B.O. and the adjutant however had their own ideas as to the location of their orderly room and chose their own abode. The Germans protested, they must use the room allotted to them; the S.B.O. remained firm and eventually the Germans gave way. But not before we had become suspicious, the proposed orderly room was searched and the microphone discovered; the Germans were NOT informed of this discovery but the camp was, and warned to take care and refrain from any conversation which would assist our hosts in any way.

16 OCTOBER 1943

By about 16 October after we had been in the camp for a week, we were extremely hungry and found the German rations quite inadequate. The camp commandant was in command of several camps and only visited ours occasionally. He made such a visit and sent in a basket of eggs to the S.B.O. who, though he must have been as hungry as any of us, promptly returned them. After breakfasting on German tea, a rumour swept through the camp that the parcels had arrived at Weinsberg station; this rumour was swiftly confirmed, and by that afternoon every officer and man had each received a Canadian Red Cross parcel and 50 cigarettes. Again we found ourselves thanking the Red Cross for their timely assistance. One officer wrote in a letter home, "Thanks to the Red Cross we do not starve." The German censor wrote on the letter "You would not have starved without the Red Cross", and the letter was returned to the writer.

The German sentries were astounded, how could England whom they believed to be very short of food allow all this food to come to us from Canada. It was difficult to convince them that every officer and man was given one such parcel every week, also 50 cigarettes a week. The German ration is supposed to be 75 cigarettes a month.

The German officers however were even more worried; they feared that we should (1) bribe the sentries with food or cigarettes and (2) store up food for use during escapes. One cannot deny that they had good grounds for such fears. They decided therefore to open the food tins themselves and dole it out to each of us in our bowls, pouring everything out of the Tins, i.e. milk, jam, meat etc., in one glorious mess. This the S.B.O. and Adjutant flatly refused to do, saying that the parcels were ours to use as directed by the Red Cross and that the Germans had nothing to do with the issue of them. (We were told all this afterwards.) Both the commandant and the S.B.O. grew very angry. The S.B.O. said "No wonder you are always having wars if all Germans are as unreasonable as you are." The commandant's reply was to the effect that we were prisoners of the Germans and would obey German orders. Finally the S.B.O. got up and delivered an ultimatum. "Very well, if you refuse to co-operate I shall not issue the parcels and I shall write to Geneva and report the whole matter to the Red Cross, and I have no doubt that counter-measures will be taken against all German P.O.Ws in England." This turned the tide of argument and finally after considerably more arguments, we were allowed to issue the parcels ourselves. The Germans however pierced all tins and searched each parcel for maps, compasses etc. In addition, to obtain our new parcel we had to return all our empty tins. For the first few weeks our hosts conscientiously searched the parcels although one officer said that he would give them 5000 marks for every illicit article that they found. The bet was a very safe one and the Germans soon grew tired of searching and eventually gave it up altogether. All they insisted upon was that we returned an empty tin for each full tin that we drew; soon we were cutting large tins in half and so getting two full tins for every single empty tin that we returned. By the time the Germans spotted this trick, we had each accumulated a reserve of empty tins, which defeated the whole object of the scheme, namely to prevent us storing up food for escapes. In addition we were always wanting tins for various purposes such as homemade "kettles", ash trays and "props" for the Theatre.

With the increase in food we all felt better and began to improve our lot so far as we could; this was difficult for our hosts regarded all our requests and suggestions with grave suspicion; we had arrived with a reputation for escaping and the Germans treated us with caution which at times showed itself as hostility.

Some description of our day must be given. Reveillé was sounded on the bugle at about 7.30 am or later. But we never knew what time the first 'count' would be; as a rule it was between 8 and 8.30, when three German soldiers would solemnly march into the camp carrying their rifles slung over their shoulders and each with a metal truncheon in his hand. They would separate and proceed towards three bells and belabour same with their truncheons:– "Ding a ding ding. Dong a dong dong. Dang a dang". This clanging meant that we were to form up on the parade ground in order to be counted. We used to form up by bungalows and 10 minutes after the bells had rung the German 'duty officer', two feldwebels and several other ranks would march on to the parade ground, while the late arrivals in various stages of undress would scuttle into the ranks or stroll insolently to their place according to character. The S.B.O. would then call the parade to attention, salute the German officers, was saluted in turn and stood the parade 'easy'. The feldwebels armed with pencil and paper would then count us – sentries were posted at various points to ensure that we did not "cook the count", while orderlies went through all the bungalows to count any "sick" including those in the hospital. After checking their figures the feldwebels would report to the German officer, we were again called to attention and then dismissed. This procedure took about 12 minutes on the average, often longer, sometimes half an hour and occurred three times every day for about 10 months when it was reduced to twice a day. Occasionally there would be a miscount and then the whole parade had to be taken all over again. On our worst day I think we had as many as five counts. As soon as we were dismissed from the morning parade there would be a rush of officers carrying large metal jugs to the top mess where these gentlemen drew tea for their respective rooms; as there are over a hundred rooms in the camp, a fairly long queue was inevitably created. The chief anxiety for the mess was caused by the uncertainty of the time of the first 'count', and hence the question "Tea before parade or after?" Often they would start serving tea, then the bells would ring and by the time the parade was over, the tea already served was cold. I must apologise for these somewhat petty domestic problems but they were our daily lot and to give a true picture of life in the camp they must be included however tedious they may be.

This tea together with German brown bread, which is very dark, sourish in taste and a trifle heavy but quite good for all that, and biscuits and "spreads" from our parcels made up one's breakfast and after 7 months as a P.O.W. one actually found it adequate provided one had retained sufficient bread from the previous day.

After breakfast our own orderlies swept out our rooms, lectures commenced, and the normal life of the camp began. Musical instruments of all kinds were played in bathrooms and W.Cs (the musicians were never allowed to practice in their own rooms), and officers walked up and down the parade ground outside; others studied or attended classes. But in the early days we were short of writing materials and text books, and often it was too cold to attend lectures in draughty rooms, so cold in fact that one had to walk up and down the parade ground to keep warm. By about 11 o'clock we would get another hot drink from the mess, usually tea or coffee. Lunch took place in two sittings at 12 and 12.30, unless the 'second count' upset the programme which it often did. One never knew when it would be held except that it would be between 11.30 am. and 3.30 pm.

During this second count our letters from home were distributed. For the first two or three months there were very few letters though the Red Cross in some miraculous way managed to sort out letters previously destined to Italy and redirect them to us in Germany – a prodigious task.

After lunch the musicians, students, idlers, walkers, talkers, lecturers, actors, lawyers, doctors, dentists, gamblers, sleepers, readers, writers etc. resumed their various roles until about 2 pm, when 'count' permitting, the 'news' was read out to those who cared to go and listen; this news consisted of translations from various German newspapers of the previous day. At 2.30 Haw Haw blared at us from the camp wireless and tea would be served from the mess to another queue of officers. Our evening meal was at about 5 or 5.30 pm, thus we had two meals in the mess, cooked centrally, comprising German rations of potatoes or barley or cabbage or sugar beet tops and a very little meat on occasions, now supplemented by food extracted from our Red Cross parcel; and three hot drinks in our own rooms. After this evening meal and as soon as it began to get dark we had our third and last 'count' from which we were dismissed to our bungalows and locked in for the night. During October 'lock-up' occurred at about 6.30 (winter time), hence we had many hours to while away at night. Later in the year, lock-up was at 4.30 pm. so that we spent 16 of each 24 hours in rooms 15 feet x 24 feet at the largest (containing the officers) or 15 x 8 feet (with 6 occupants).

Such was our 'day' and from the first, the S.B.O. and adjutant strove to have the 'counts' at fixed times so as not to dislocate the daily programme of meals, classes, concerts etc. The Germans refused to agree to this demand saying that if they had the parade at fixed times it would be easier for us to time our escapes; they did however agree not to have them during our meals.

Next we asked that we should not be locked in until "lights out at 10.30 pm" – this also was refused. 'Lock up' was a standing order of the O.K.W. (Ober-Kommander Wehrmacht) and applied to all prison camps throughout Germany.

Lastly we asked that we might be allowed out on walks; this too was refused, even though we offered to give our parole. Many times was this request repeated, but it was not granted until the following spring.

Sequel: Letter to John – Moosburg and Liberation

Perry Orchard, Wingham, Canterbury CT3 1ER
Telephone: Canterbury (0227) 720236

Date: 16th March 1992

Dear John,

Thanks very much for the loan of your P.O.W. Log Book, one of the girls in the office took two photocopies of the relevant items, so I am now returning the Log Book together with one set of photocopies which I have numbered in red ink; and typed copies of 'Room Six' and 'A Study in Morbid Psychology'– this implies no disrespect to your handwriting, but is an admission that my eyesight is not as good as it used to be. I overheard some female laughter whilst these historic documents were being typed!! Lastly, I have now discovered my own P.O.W. Log Book and photocopies of that are also enclosed in a separate bundle in which the photos are identified by letters in alphabetical order.

All this has reawakened my interest in those historic days; I think you told me that you were 'taken' when Tobruk was captured by Rommel's Africa Corps on 20th June 1942 and soon afterwards you and all the other P.O.W.s were handed over to the Italians for imprisonment; it would be interesting to know how you were transported to Modena. I was with the First Army in Tunisia on about the 23rd March 1943, thanks to some Arabs, I was captured by the Hermann Goering Division whilst on a night patrol behind their lines; taken to a large disused rubber factory in Tunis where there were many other P.O.W.s – some from the Eighth Army captured at or just prior to the Battle of the Mareth Line; a week or so later a thousand or so more of us were handed over to Italian Guards and escorted onto an Italian ship, with an Italian crew but German A.A. Gunners; we were all herded down into the hold and taken to Livorno (formerly known as Leghorn) during that sea trip the pangs of hunger were at their worst – I expect you had the same experience – and there was an endless queue to go up on deck for a breath of fresh air and a visit to a very insanitary loo. At Liverno our heads were shaven and we were given some food (mostly dry dusty bread) and put on a passenger train (not cattle trucks) for Capua – P.G. 66 which was overlooked by Mount Vesuvius. That camp was very primitive and the Italian Guards were "trigger happy" but it was there that we received our first Red Cross food pack (a Canadian one) the food supplied by our captors was meagre and nauseating.

Towards the end of April or early in May we were put in a train of cattle trucks for Modena in time for some special food on Easter Day and a liberal supply of Marsalce wine!! I think it was a week or so before the Sports; we were all very impressed to see how well you chaps had organised the camp and learnt that the previous winter had been such a lean time; that each of you were saving up tinned food as a reserve for the coming winter and we were advised to do the same.

Sicily was invaded on 10th July and finally fell on 12th August; Italy was invaded during the night 9th–10th September 1943 and by 16th September "The Toe" had been captured and Bari was taken on 22/23rd September. I think it was on or about 15th September that the S.B.O. "Colonel De Beers" informed us secretly that Italy was likely to surrender very soon and his orders were that we were not – "REPEAT NOT" to try to escape; you may remember that soon afterwards our Italian Guards deserted; those on our "Pommies" side of the camp ran into a field of maize, where they must have dumped their arms and uniforms and emerged later as civilians. Can you remember the date when this happened? 16th September? After that there were rumours that the Camp would be taken over by the Germans and under pressure the S.B.O. relented a bit by saying that he would not hinder P.O.W.s who could not speak Italian from trying to escape – many tried to do so and I believe a few of them were successful, but most of them were caught by the Hermann Goering Division which surrounded the camp and posted very competent armed guards who left us in no doubt that anyone who tried to escape would be shot. They were the same people who had captured me in North Africa.

You may remember that a day or so later we were warned to make ourselves ready to be moved into Germany and would only be permitted to take such food and clothing as we could carry; so the question arose as to what to do with the large stock of food held in reserve for the winter – we did not want the Germans to have it, so we started throwing it over the barbed wire to the Italian peasants and farm workers because we had reason to believe that they were hungry and also we hoped that by so doing we might induce some of them to help any escaped P.O.W. whom they met. The Italians were delighted, although some of their children were hurt by tins of cheese and other food; they gathered in their crowds and unwisely cheered us; that of course angered the Germans; their guards warned us that they would shoot anyone who threw any more food over the fence. I expect you chaps had a similar experience. I remember that during the following night any surplus food was burnt. I think it was probably on or about 22nd September that we marched to the Railway Station and boarded a long train of Cattle trucks and open goods wagons; my party were crowded into a Cattle truck where there was just – but only just – enough room for each of us to lie down on the strawed floor – we were protected from the weather but could not see much of the country-side. As I recall we had a slow journey of about 139 miles (according to my atlas) to Bolzano where we were permitted to disembark for a few minutes in the late evening; then we travelled another 60 odd miles to Innsbruck where we again disembarked in the early morning for a much needed bath in a cold mountain stream – I liked the look of the town so much that I vowed to return there after the war, I did so several times. There followed a much slower journey to Munich about 120 miles and I believe it was during that journey that young Lord Brabourne of the Grenadier Guards tried to escape from an open wagon and was shot dead by the guards; do you know any more about this incident? From Munich we travelled to Moosburg, which I think was another 20 miles or so – it is not shown on my atlas – there, you will remember, was a huge P.O.W. camp; which contained thousands of Russians and – alas, millions of lice, bed bugs, fleas and other vermin; but very little food and no Red Cross parcels. Fortunately we did not stay there very long; one of the German Officers told me, "We are going to move you to a new Oflag near Heilbronn where you will all be much more comfortable". When we moved there was the usual long train of cattle trucks which contained rea-sonably clean straw for us to lie on, but we were all so infested by vermin that sleep was well nigh impossible; in fact we were taken to Strasbourg (about 243 miles) – where we were able to have a cold but very necessary wash and given a chance to get rid of some of our vermin before march-ing to "Fort Bismark" where we were imprisoned for a week or more

– "because your new camp is not quite ready". You may remember that there were two or three ingenious and successful escapes from that Fort, and it was one or two days before the Germans realised what happened; because although we were counted three or four times a day; several people feigned illness and were counted separately in the "sick bay" and then managed to join the main body of P.O.W.s to be counted again. The food was a bit better than at Moosburg (it could not have been worse) but there were no Red Cross parcels and we were all "b....y hungry"! I think it was early in October that we marched down to the Railway Station and once again boarded a train of Cattle trucks to travel about 110 miles to Heilbronn then another 5 or 6 miles to Weinsberg (which is not shown on my atlas) and it was a short march to the camp where there was an ample supply of cold water for washing and delousing. I think it was about 20th October '43 that we moved into Oflag[1] V.A. and I believe that it was another month before the first Red Cross parcels were delivered. The meagre ration of German bread and potatoes only whetted our appetites and all of us were still "b....y hungry" – my body weight was about 133 lbs (compared to my normal weight of 182 lbs).

I expect you remember that 1943/4 was a very cold winter, the thermometer outside our bungalow registered –11°Centigrade; but our fuel ration, if carefully used was just sufficient to keep our rooms warm in the evenings; during that winter our entertainment was very limited to listening to a gramophone, reading, playing card games and attending talks and lectures, especially those by Dimbleby, after he had studied the newspapers; I remember him telling us about the Battle of Azio in January 1944 and the speculations in the German Newspapers about the "Second Front". I am not sure when you "musical boys" obtained your instruments, which I believe were supplied by the Red Cross and/or the Y.M.C.A. – but I see that your photo of The Revellers is dated May 1944 and "Old John" – 30.6.44.

The first of the Walks – "on parole" which I joined was on 3rd April 1944. I joined 24 more walks, the last on 27.12.44, I had signed the list for three further walks, on 26th March, 19th and 23rd April 1944 but these were cancelled.

---

[1]   Oflag: shortened form of German Offizierslager, meaning 'Officer's Camp'.

I think it was on or about 1st June 1945 that Dimbleby told us the German Newspapers reported that the allied invasion was imminent and would almost certainly be in "The Pas de Calais" – which you and I now know, is exactly what the allies wanted them to think; due to bad weather D. Day was postponed till 5th June; we heard something about it the next day on the 7th. Dimbleby was able to confirm the news. Our hopes rose but we knew there would be some desperate fighting before the allies could establish a bridgehead and launch a full scale attack. It was about 20th August that Dimbleby told us that the allies had broken through "The Falaise Gap"; a week or so later he told us that Paris had been occupied by General De Gaule. The news that was most pleasing to me (and others who had been in the B.E.F. (British Expeditionary Force) in 1940 and evacuated from Dunkirk) was that the Germans had retired from Brussels which was occupied by the Guards Armoured Division on 4th September; I think we heard about it a few days later.

By this time – September 1944 – the war in the air was often above our heads, I am sure you remember those daylight raids by hundreds of American "Flying Fortresses" their 'fire power' was so intense that when they remained "in formation" the German Fighter Planes were "outgunned" and we saw several shot down; during the night it was the R.A.F.s turn they bombed Stuttgart many times, and Heilbronn which was far too close for comfort, I was told that their heavy bombers "Lancaster" carried extra 'bomb-racks' which would be discarded after the bombs they had carried. Sure enough one of those metal racks nearly killed me one night, a long springy piece of metal landed close to me when we were ordered to "take cover" in the slit trenches, it bounced high into the air and thinking it was an unexploded bomb I beat a very hasty retreat! The camp was covered with masses of thin paper like strips, which you may remember was known as "window" used to confuse the German Radar.

As the bombing intensified we became more and more apprehensive about our own safety; then someone said that one of the "Pommies" had received a letter from his brother in the R.A.F. advising him to study religion whilst he was a P.O.W. – particularly the Psalm 91 Verse 5 – "This must be a code" said the recipient, so he looked up the text – it reads "Thou shalt not be afraid for any terror that flieth by night" – did you hear that story John? Those of us who did were delighted "the R.A.F. must know where we are" – later I became a bit doubtful because no one could tell me the name of the officer concerned.

On our walks during the autumn of 1944 some of us picked large quantities of Blackberries; and a few others decided to use them to make some Blackberry wine for Christmas; this would be given to those of us who had supplied the berries and the sugar needed for wine making; sugar was in short supply and the Vinters warned us that the wine would be "very dry", it proved to be so acid that no one could drink it; so some bright New Zealander suggested that the wine should be distilled into "Blackberry Brandy". I did not see the distilling apparatus but I was told that "Heath Robinson" would have been proud of it; eventually the Brandy was made and it was decided that a tough bushwhacker fellow should sample it "Smutsy" was considered to be just the person and he readily agreed to drink some of the Brandy. You probably knew him, he can be seen in my photo E2, Middle row, left end. He drank several mouthfuls of the stuff and then "passed out" completely!! Two British M.O.s were hastily summoned, and after sniffing the Brandy, tasting a sip of it, burning a spoonful of it they said it was probably "Wood Alcohol" and added that Smutsy might go blind or suffer D.T.S. – "Burn the stuff it is poisonous". Thankfully Smutsy recovered alright and the Brandy burnt with a bright flame. Did you hear about this incident?

On Christmas Day 1944 bets were being made as to whether we should be freed by 1st May 1945; I bet Brian Lax that we would but later I thought I had been too optimistic. You may remember that early in March 1945, the Americans captured a bridge over the Rhine (about a fortnight before the main assault) and a day or two later we noticed that some of our guards were slightly drunk and in the town below us we could see there were some celebrations; by that time we had got to know some of the Guards personally – "Otto, are you drunk on parade? And what are the people of Weinsberg celebrating?" Otto grinned owlishly "You haf 'eard the Americans haf crossed the Rhine?" "Yes, yes we know all about that", "Well we are not going to let them drink our beautiful wine, so we shall drink it all before they get 'ere".

Once again the S.B.O. warned us not to try to escape, "If you did you would simply become one of a million 'displaced persons' and find it impossible to prove your identity to any one in authority".

A week or so later we were warned to make ready to be moved by train; by this time the Germans were so scared of the Russians that they were only too ready to comply with the wishes of the S.B.O. – who insisted that a large party of P.O.W.s should be taken down to the station to prepare the train which was being assembled to move us – you may have been one of that party; large Red Crosses on a white background were painted on the rooves of some of the cattle trucks and the letters P.O.W. were painted in large capitals on the others. That train became the only safe haven from numerous American and R.A.F. planes. Also we were allowed to take stacks of food on our journey.

The German Camp Commandant bid us all quite a friendly farewell, I remember him saying that the numerous efforts to escape had nearly driven him mad but he had enjoyed attending all the functions to which he and his officers had been invited.

I think we boarded the train on or about 29th March and had a very slow journey back to Moosburg; we stopped quite frequently sometimes for several hours; frequently fighter bombers would dive down towards our train and then peel off without harming us. Local people noticed this and clustered alongside our train. At Munich the numerous Railway Sidings were cluttered with Steam Engines which had obviously been "shot up" by allied planes; finally we reached Moosburg (on or about 2nd April) and after standing for about six hours or so, we "Pommies" were admitted to a hot shower room; I think your lot got there before us. The Camp was larger and even more crowded than before, but here as at Weinsberg the Germans tried to be helpful, they were very frightened about the Russians.

During the next two weeks or so air activity increased and the sounds of warfare grew even closer; these were limited to small local battles. After the Allies had crossed the Rhine in force (23/24th March) – and as we now know Montgomery's 21st Army Group had occupied most of Holland (18th April) and the American troops under Generals Patton and Bradley were advancing eastwards – the German will to resistance was ended; there was only "token resistance" to the relentless pressure of the allied armies. Many more P.O.W.s came to Moosburg whilst we were there; large numbers had been compelled to march a long way from camps in Eastern Germany which had been hastily vacated before being overrun by the Russians; these included allied soldiers whose morale was still pretty good; they were obviously very tired but gave us a grin and the "Thumbs Up" sign when we cheered them as they entered the camp; despite their ordeal most of them were shaven and had retained their self respect. Quite a lot of recently captured American soldiers were also brought into the camp; many of them looked very scruffy; "Why bother to wash and shave just to impress the Huns" said one of their junior officers named Hank; I think it was "Arthur Duveen" a regular Cavalry Officer – who was always shaved and dressed as well as possible – who simply said "Watch" and he marched up to a German Sentry who promptly stood to attention and gave a smart salute; Arthur returned the salute and turned to Hank "That's why" he said. Hank laughed "O.K." he said "lend me a razor".

Munich was occupied peacefully on 30th April and I think it must have been the next day that a small American Task Force entered the camp after a minor skirmish in the early morning; I heard that one of three tanks smashed its way through the Main Entrance gate in true "Hollywood Fashion"; the. P.O.W.s who witnessed the incident all cheered and the German Officers and Guards surrendered or deserted. This was followed by an anti climax; the American Officer in charge said that it would be two or three days before we could be released and during that time we must remain in the camp – "If you stray from the camp you will become 'displaced persons' and anyone caught looting may be shot"; an hour or so later we "Pommies" were posted as Sentries around the outside of the camp with orders to stop the Russians or any other P.O.W.s from getting out and looting!! Of course it was an impossible task, we were not armed and as if by magic gaping holes were made in the barbed wire perimeter fence and soon there were queues of escapees, mostly Russians.

The American C.O. appreciated our difficulties and simply said "Well, when they come back lead them to our guard room if you can"; that evening one small and very drunk Russian staggered up to the holes I was supposed to be guarding; he was blissfully happy "Kriegs Furtig – Yah?" – "Yah" I replied and taking him by the arm I escorted him towards the Guard room; he did not try to resist but tried to persuade me to have a drink from the bottle he was carrying – probably Schnapps or something similar – then he passed out so I had to carry him to the Guard room where I was rewarded with a packet of American Cigarettes – "Lucky Strike". A day or so later General Patton himself visited the camp – I did not see him but I was told that he was armed with his famous pearl-studded pistols and said "We must get these Guys out of this rat hole very soon".

The next day a large contingent of American "supply troops" arrived armed with powder–blowers with which they disinfected us with D.D.T. and large supplies of food – nothing fancy but large quantities of

American white bread, on which numerous "artistes" spread large dollops of jam (or peanut butter) with a spoon. A day or so later we were driven to Landshut Airfield where hundreds of Dakota Planes were lined up on either side of the grass runway. The planes had been used by parachutists in battle and on our plane these words appeared over the entrance door "Abandon hope all ye who enter here". We were flown to Brussels, where on 8th May we heard that peace had been declared. The whole town went mad with delight; never have I seen so many people crowded onto the rooves, bonnets and running boards of buses. The next day we Pommies were flown in Dakotas to Abbevile where we were transferred to R.A.F. Lancasters and flown to Wing Airfield, I believe that the South African and New Zealanders or some of them were flown to Manston and housed in a holiday camp at Margate before being returned to their home countries.

Sorry to burden you with this lot but my school teacher daughter has often urged me to write about my experiences as a P.O.W. and two of my grand daughters have done the same. Perhaps you ought to become a historian too.

> With all best wishes,
> *Frank Elgar*

The History of Moosburg Camp[1]

HISTORY

The camp was opened in September 1939 and was designed to house up to 10,000 Polish prisoners from the German September 1939 offensive. The first prisoners arrived while the wooden barracks were under construction and for several weeks lived in tents.

British, French, Belgian and Dutch soldiers taken prisoner during the Battle of France started arriving in May 1940. Many were transferred to other camps, but close to 40,000 French remained at Stalag VII-A throughout the war.

British, Greek and Yugoslavian prisoners arrived from the Balkans Campaign in May and June 1941. A few months later Soviet prisoners started arriving, mostly officers. At the end of the war there were 27 Soviet generals in the prison.

More British Commonwealth and Polish prisoners came from the North African campaign and the offensive against the Italian-held islands in the Mediterranean. They were brought from Italian POW camps after the Armistice with Italy in September 1943, including many who escaped at that time and were recaptured. Italian soldiers were also imprisoned.

The first American arrivals came after the Tunisia Campaign in December 1942, and the Italian Campaign in 1943. Large numbers of Americans were captured in the Battle of the Bulge in December 1944.

Among the last arrivals were officers from Stalag Luft III who had been force-marched from Sagan in Silesia (now Żagań), Poland). They arrived on 2 February 1945. They were followed by more prisoners marched from other camps threatened by the advancing Soviets, including American officers who had been marched from Oflag 64 in Szubin, via Oflag XIII-B, under their senior officer Lt.Col. Paul Goode.

---

[1]   Source: https://en.wikipedia.org/wiki/Stalag_VII-A

During the 5 and a half years about 1,000 prisoners died at the camp, over 800 of them Soviets. They were buried in a cemetery in Oberreit, south of Moosburg. Most died from illness, some from injuries during work.

On 1 August 1942 Major Karl August Meinel was shifted into the Führerreserve, because on 13 January 1942 he wrote a critical report to General Hermann Reinecke on the segregation and execution of Russian prisoners of war in Stalag VII-A by the Gestapo and the Sicherheitsdienst SD (security service) of the Reichsführer SS (Heinrich Himmler).

LIBERATION

Stalag VII-A was captured on 29 April 1945 by Combat Command A of the 14th Armored Division. A German proposal for an armistice was rejected, followed by a short, uneven battle between the American tanks and retreating German soldiers for control of bridges across the Amper and Isar rivers. The German contingent included "remnants of the 17th SS Panzer Grenadier and 719th Infantry Divisions...which had no tanks or antitank guns, and were armed with only small arms, machine guns, mortars, and panzerfausts". Large numbers surrendered, as did the camp's 240 guards. The American force learned of the existence of the camp and its approximate location only a few hours before the attack. Because so many Allied POWs were in the area, the U.S. artillery, a major factor in any attack, was ordered not to fire, and remained silent during the attack. According to official German sources, there had been 76,248 prisoners at the camp in January 1945.

AFTERMATH

After the liberation Stalag VII-A was turned into Civilian Internment Camp #6 for 12,000 German men and women suspected of criminal activity for the Nazi regime. Later the camp was turned into a new district of the town called Moosburg-Neustadt.

A memorial to inmates of Stalag VII-A was built. It is a fountain located in the centre of Neustadt. It consists of four bas-reliefs created out of local stone by the French sculptor Antoniucci Volti [fr] while he was a prisoner in the camp.

In 1958 the Oberreit cemetery was closed. 866 bodies were exhumed and reburied at the military cemetery in Schwabstadl near Landsberg. The bodies of 33 Italians were reburied at the Italian Memorial Cemetery near Munich. In 1982 the Moosburg City Council purchased a plot at the site of the old Oberreit cemetery and erected a wooden cross with a simple stone remembering the dead of Stalag VII-A.

"Repatriated"[1]

F.E. ELGAR left Eagle House in December, 1930, for Tonbridge. He was an articled surveyor from 1935-39 and was commissioned in the Sherwood Forresters in 1940. He was evacuated from Dunkirk on June 1st, 1940, and was captured very shortly after landing in N. Africa in December, 1942. We quote in full from a letter he wrote on his return to England to Mr. and Mrs. Thorp:-

"Thanks very much for your telegram: I have been home just a week now and as you can well imagine I have thoroughly enjoyed it. I wrote to you and also Mr. Lockhart while I was a prisoner and often wonder if the letters reached their destinations.

We were liberated from Stalag VII. A., at Moosburg near Munich, on Sunday, April 29th. There were over 30,000 prisoners there, as the Germans had moved us and other camps to Moosburg during the previous month. The camp was about fifteen miles North-East of Munich and we were liberated by the American Third Army - "Patton's boys" as they called themselves - after a very short fight by the Germans. Patton himself visited the camp a few days later and though I did not see him personally, I hear that he wore a beautiful pair of pearl-handled pistols, and remarked that they would get us out of this rat-hole as soon as possible.

Bad weather delayed our return to England, but we eventually left the camp on May 7th and were driven to a near-by aerodrome; about 2,000 were flown off that day, but my party did not leave until the next day. We were flown to Rheims in an American Dakota D47; being a troop-carrying plane, we had ample room and comfortable seats and could see perfectly; the weather was fine and we had a most enjoyable trip, passing over Stuttgart, Metz, and Verdun en route. From Rheims we were directed to another town fifty miles away, and after re-fuelling we did the trip in twenty minutes; but again we were not expected and were

---

[1]   An extract from a newsletter from Eagle House School, which Frank Elgar Attended in the 1930's.

told to make for Brussels. Before we left, however, the Americans drove up to our plane in jeeps with white bread, jam, pickles, cheese, tomato juice, and tea, which they offered us with such liberality that even the hungriest were satisfied, and we staggered back to our plane, feeling very replete. On our way to Brussels darkness began to fall and we could see rockets, fireworks and Verey lights being fired in the towns and villages and guessed that Victory celebrations had started. We landed at Brussels on a huge aerodrome and were received in a hangar by English W.V.S.[2] and dear old N.A.A.F.I.[3] who gave us more tea, cigarettes, chocolate and biscuits. Then we bid good-bye to our pilot and were driven through a crowded and rejoicing town to our quarters. Although it was now nearly almost midnight, the Canadian reception committee dealt with us at once; we were sprayed with "de-lousing" powder (un-necessary in my case I assure you), issued with kit, given an advance of pay, more cigarettes, chocolate, etc., had a shower and finally a meal and at last got to bed at three a.m., but I was up again at seven, being too excited to sleep much. At mid-day we were driven to the aerodrome again and many were flown home; our party however were unlucky as the weather took an unfavourable turn. So we returned to our quarters and that night several of us visited the town. The central square and streets were crowded with rejoicing people and allied soldiers; we at last managed to get a table outside a cafe where we sat and watched the crowds, aided by a bottle of Sauterne - the waiter himself had been a P.O.W. and did all he could for us. We did not get back until two a.m. and a notice on each door informed us of an early start, reveille at five a.m. Thus we were somewhat weary the following morning, but this time all went well, and we flew home in a Lancaster and landed at Wing near Aylesbury. England looked marvellous as we were driven to a camp at Chalfont St. Giles; here we filled in forms, were issued with ration cards and telephoned home and arrived here the following day.

Aunt Marian[4] has the magazine, so I hope to get all the school news. I was in the same room as a chap who was at the Dragon School and we became great friends, and I met another from St. Neots. We have been allowed double rations, and I am taking full advantage of it and am none

---

2   W.V.S., Women's Voluntary Service.
3   N.A.A.F.I., Navy, Army and Air Force Institutes.
4   Marian Elgar, Frank's Aunt who lived at Crockshard Farm, Wingham.

the worse for it. Compared with other prisoners we have been very lucky, some of them have had an appalling time."

Epilogue to The War Diaries of Frank Elgar

Frank very rarely spoke about his war experience. As a strong Christian, he was always insistent on the need to forgive.

On his return to the family home at Dene Farm, one of his first actions was to hire a new worker for the farm … a former German POW named Otto, a man who became much respected in the local community. Frank's wife Mary frequently commented on how Otto worked much harder than his English colleagues!

Several years later, the Elgar family paid a brief visit to Weinsberg, where the camp was resplendent with mature trees planted during the time when Frank was held prisoner. To the consternation of Frank (and the amusement of his family!) it was then being used as a holiday camp!

Appendix 1: Addresses of POW fellow inmates

W.A. Place
5, Streathbourne Rd
Balham SW17
London

J.C. Wright
The Cottage,
Tushingham
Whitchurch. Shropshire

C.M. Mould
5, Palace Green
Addington
Surrey

Tel: Museum   62865201
c/o Robt Heurtahand– Ltd.
20 Bernes St W1

G. Long
Transit Valley Country Club
Buffalo
New York
USA

Home Address:

501 3½ Street
S.W.
Ronuk, Virginia
U.S.A.

Sergeant Hodgekinson,
Hawthorns
Noose
Willenhall, Staffs

Corporal Bates
16 Renishaw Rd
Martin Moor
Chesterfield, Derbyshire

Pte Ratcliffe,
Tunedin
1 Melton Rd
West Bridgeford
Nottingham

P.W. Weightman
1 Crarka Road
Deanham
Maryport
Cumb

Marlins Bank, Rennoth
Tel: Rennoth 296 (Officer)

L.B. Young
Mount Pleasant, Kilekeggan
Dunbartonshire, Scotland

Pte Crossley,
31 Overend Rd,
Worksop.
Notts.

Appendix 2: Books for future reference

English Farming Past and Present, Lord Emle (A.E. Protheroe)

Soil & Sense

What the Church Teaches, The Bishop of Bradford

Look to the Land, Lord

The Living Soil, C.B. Balfour

The English Countryman, Maningham

England their England, A.G. Macdonnell

Short Stories, L. Tolstoy

Rasselus, Johnson
   Hilaire Belloc's criticism of this book is a strong recommendation to read it.

BOOKS – CAPUA

This is an incomplete list of some of the books that I have read in captivity and does NOT include (a) text books (b) books that I had already read before being captured, e.g. those of Dorothy Sayers.
   (Commenced 3 Dec. 44 Weinsberg)
   Mostly from memory.

Capua

Very limited supplies

Nancy Stair, Eleanor MacCartney Lane
   (More of a poetess – Burns – fair only)

The Bridge at San Luis Rey, Thornton Wilder

Well written – 7 people killed by collapse of bridge. The story of each. Good but not up to my expectations.

The Flying Bosun, Arthur Mason
Sea novel – tinge of superstition, enjoyed it.

BOOKS – MODENA

Modena

Excellent library, cannot hope to remember all that I have read here.

The Gentleman of the Party, A.G. Street
A very fine character study of genuine farm labourer – stockman; a good historical picture of farming conditions before, during and after the War (14–18). An excellent book.

The House under the Water

Oliver Twist (1838), Charles Dickens – 1812–1870

The Three Musketeers, Dumas

Murder must Advertise, D.L. Sayers
One of the few Peter Wimsey stories that was still new to me. Enjoyed it immensely. Very instructive re advertising business; again impressed by her knowledge and description of details.

Trader Horn

How Green was my Valley, Richard Llewellyn
The story of [Huw] son of a Welsh miner, and the green valley in which the mine was sunk slowly ruined by the dumps of waste etc. Absorbingly interesting and very moving – compare The Stars Look Down. No wonder the miners became bitter.

Many of us ransacked the library before leaving Modena, and by swapping, borrowing etc. I read a few books in the tedious time of moving.

The Country House, John Galsworthy

Poe

R.L. Stephenson

BOOKS – WEINSBERG

The Library commenced with about 600 Books which we had brought with us (between about 1300 officers). Thanks to Red Cross, Y.M.C.A. and private books on loan, it now consists of about 8000 volumes, fiction and non-fiction – v. well catalogued. List entirely from memory, no particular order.

A Passage to India, E.M. Forster
A very good and illuminating story of India. The British snobbishness towards the Indian brilliantly and mercilessly exposed. Dr. Aziz, Mrs Moore and Mr Fielding and Miss Quested and of course The Turtons.

Howards End, E.M. Forster
Art, beauty, kindness – business methods, the latter partially defended as at being necessary at present. Beautifully written. Liked it better than the above.

All Passion Spent, V. Sackville-West
Reminded me of Howards End but earlier period (late Edwardian) beautifully written too. The story of a Lady.

Orphan Island, Rose Macaulay

Told by an Idiot

Crewe Train

The Mill on the Floss, George Eliot (Mary Ann or Marian Cross née Evans)
Written 1860
Beautiful descriptions and study of rural life of about 1800
Characters: Maggie and Tom Tulliver

Adam Bede (1859) Not so good as the above but I very much enjoyed it.
Characters: Hetty; Arthur Donnithorne; Mr Irwine (the rector); Dinah (Weslyan preacher portrait of G.E.s Aunt); Seth Bede (G.E.s Uncle); Bartle Massey (school master); Mrs Poyser (G.E.s Mother); Mr Poyser (Tenant Farmer).

Silas Marner (1861), George Eliot – Period 1800

Story: S.M. unjustly accused of theft in London, goes to Raveloe becomes a miner lives alone by weaving. He is robbed but finds and adopts a child of a strange woman who dies on his doorstep, calls the child Eppie. Helped by Dolly Winthrop a wheelwright's wife. The dead mother is revealed as wife of Godfrey Cass the Squire's son. SM's money stolen by Dunstan Cass who is then drowned. Body and money discovered. Godfrey after bearing the load of guilty knowledge forgiven by and marries Nancy Lammeter. Eppie marries. All happy etc.

Greenacres (1800), Doreen Wallace
Same period as above. Suffolk countryside. Effects of enclosure. Trials of rural population. Very interesting and well told.

George Meredith

Fielding

Anthony Trollope

Essays etc.

Montaigne

Hazlitt

Aldous Huxley

Charles Lamb

Bacon

Emerson

G.K. Chesterton

Selected Essays, Hilaire Belloc

R.L. Stephenson

Short Stories, L. Tolstoy

Is Christianity True?, C.E.M. Joad and A. Lunn
All the problems of belief thrashed out in letters between these two scholars. Joad rather illogical and frivolous – Lunn answers the problems admirably.

King Ludwig I of Bavaria

My Struggle, Adolph Hitler
ZENTRALVERLAG DER NSDAP. FRANZ NACHF, G.M.B.H.
I commenced reading this book 28 Jan 45 – the day after the author announced that the Russians were 100 miles from Berlin.
Finished it on 5 March 45 – by which time the Russians were within 25 miles of Berlin, on the Oder.
Interesting but rather heavy going. Struck by Hitler's contempt for the intelligence of the masses; his logical but narrow minded arguments and conclusions and the way in which he has since copied the very methods that he condemns as used by the Marxists and Jews.

She Married Pushkin

The Brothers Karamazov, Dostoevsky

Aldous Huxley

The Wallet of Kai Lung

Kai Lung's Golden Hours

R. L. Stephenson.

Faster! Faster!, E.M. Delafield
Very readable. Interesting character and psychological studies.

Captain Nicholas, Hugh Walpole
The Captain is a bounder. Invades a solid family and causes trouble, finally evicted by the mother. Interesting and in parts v. moving. Funny.

The Green Mirror

The Hunchback of Notre Dame, Victor Hugo

Farmer's Story, A.G. Street

Silver Ley, Adrian Bell

The Farmer in New Zealand, Alley and Hall. 11–12 March 45.
A short but interesting history of farming in New Zealand – shows strikingly how adaptive they are to changing demand and new methods

introduced by scientific discovery particularly – refrigeration, electric power and the centrifugal milk separator.

Interesting to compare this industrialised farming with that advocated by Lord Northborne, whose book Look to the Land is quoted. Note that co-operative methods of production and selling secure to the N.Z. Farmer 85% of the retails price of his products.

Mystery Ships, J.S. Brian

Relates the facts and the many fables concerned with the disappearance of the *Marie Celeste* – originally *The Amazon*. Launched 18 May 1861 – a half or Schooner Brig – built by Joshua Davis at Spencer Island, Parrsbarro – Nova Scotia. Wrecked in 1867 – rechristened in 1868 the *Marie Celeste* after salvage, muddle over new registration.

On Tuesday 5 Nov, 1812 left New York (after extensive repairs) for Mediterranean, Captain Benjamin Briggs in command, his wife and child on board. Cargo alcohol. Captain, steady, serious, teetotaller. Found abandoned on Dec 5, 1812 between 1 and 2 pm nautical time (civil time pm 4 Dec) by Capt Morehouse of the *Dei Gratia*; sea-worthy, all ship shape, ships papers and 1 chronometer missing. Log book completed up to 21 Nov – weather fine, sea calm from that date till 5 Dec.

Many stories as to causes of disappearance, all enlarged on or distorted the facts including A.C. Doyle (Arthur Conan Doyle) under the name of J. Habakuk Jephson – Cornhill's Magazine 1884 – but a dozen other writers did the same including J.G. Lockhart Mysteries of the Sea 1925 which I believe I read at Tenbridge.

The Keys of the Kingdom, A.J. Cronin.

The story of an R.C. missionary; from his boyhood in Scotland, to China and his work on his return to Scotland. Francis is almost too good to believe. Thoroughly enjoyed it.

The Citadel

Doctor Manson who commenced in a Welsh mining village and eventually after a hard struggle does well in London. Gives way to the demands of money and selfishness until he loves his wife (not Denny as in the film) Christine.

Most enjoyable. But Taffy tells me he is unjust to the profession.

The Stars Look Down

Martin Chuzzlewit, Charles Dickens

Appendix 3: Gramophone records

1 *Handel's Water Music*

2 *Jesu joy of man's desiring* – Bach. Cantata No 24?
(Probably only 'Piano' recording – try and get orchestral if possible, piano alone weak.)

3 *Mozart's Serenade*
Einer Kleiner Nacht music (a little night music)

Appendix 4: Menu, songs, etc

Menu

Consommé Froid
ooo
Saumon Sauce Mayonnaise
Petits Pois Verts
ooo
Tranche de Porc Mayfair
Sauce Vinaigrette
ooo
Gelée aux Fruits Hiller
ooo
Café frappé noir
ooo
Petits Fours

THE MANAGEMENT REGRET THE ABSENCE OF
KNIVES OWING TO WARTIME
RESTRICTIONS

FOLLOW THE VAN.

My old man says follow the van,
And don't dilly dally on the way,
Off goes the van with my home
packed in it,
And I walk behind with my old
cock Linnet,
And I dillies and dallies –
dallies and dillies,
Lost my way and don't know where
to roam,
And I stop behind to have my old
half quartern,
And I can't find my way home.

+++++++++++++++++

DIRLY DIRL.

For I'm on-ly a 'ittle dir-ly dirl,
A innocent 'ittle dir-ly dirl,
Ev'wy hour in the day
Twying hard to o-bey
My dear-west, my sweetest ma-ma.

+++++++++++

OFLAG V--A. MUSIC FOR CHRISTMAS DAY

HOCH und DEITSCH–	
MEISTER – MARCH	...Dominik Ertl
DANSE MOLDAVE –	
AIR DE BALLET	...Georges Razigade
VILLA from	
MERRY WIDOW	...Franz Léhar
SERENADE A MARI–	
NETTE – MORCEAU	
DE GENRE	...Max Sheimbet
MINUET IN "A"	...L. Boccherini
COEUR AFFOLÉ.	
ROMANZA APPAS–	
SIONATO	...F.D. Marchetti
PIZZI–PUZZI –	
PIZZIKATO–STÄND–	
CHEN	...Herman Krome
SO KOMMEN SIE, from	
MERRY WIDOW	...Franz Léhar
SERENADE	...G. Pierné
REVE APRES LE	
BAL – SCHERZO	...Ed. Broustet
DOINA VODA –	
DANSE ROUMAINE	...de Maurizi
FATME – INTER–	
MEZZO ORIENTAL	...Jul Dworzak
MANNEQUIN – IN–	...A. Pickert
TERMEZZO	
PARADE OF THE TIN	
SOLDIERS : MARCH	...Léon Jessel

MINIATURE ORCHESTRA
under the direction
of Leonard Inskip

Appendix 5: Illustrations, Photographs and Maps

Frank Elgar, 1942/3

Frank Elgar's POW ID Card

Frank Elgar's Movements as a POW

The Officers of the 2ⁿᵈ Batallion, The Sherwood Foresters, c.1942

Oflag V.A.

Standing: Callam Morrison, Derek Lane, Frank Elgar, Ray Lever, Lucky Young & I.K. Nixon. *Seated*: Ted Edwards, Derek Nimmo-Smith, M.B. Davies, Clifford Mould

Postcard, 17th May 1944

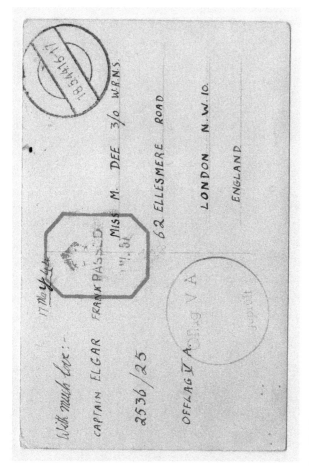

Postcard, 17th May 1944

Oflag V.A. Weinsberg, July 1944

I.K.Nixon, D. Lane, J. De Klerk, F. Elgar, M.B. Davies, M.N. Smiut, D.B. Edwards, H.W. Le Marchant, C.M. Mould, L.B. Young, T. Weightman, S.J. Vanrensburg, M. Nimmo-Smith

Grouse in June

Grouse in June

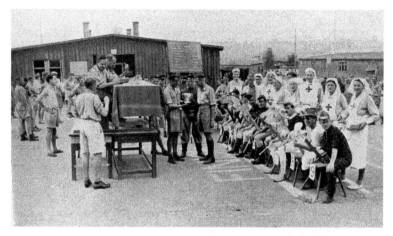

Oflag V.A. Weinsberg

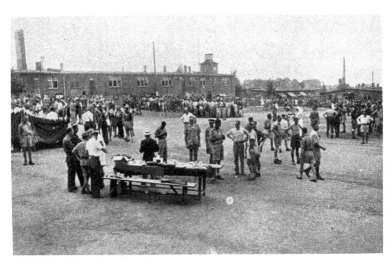

Oflag V.A. Weinsberg

Oflag V.A. Weinsberg

May 1943

Modena, May 1943

Moosburg, Bavaria

www.ingramcontent.com/pod-product-compliance
Ingram Content Group UK Ltd.
Pitfield, Milton Keynes, MK11 3LW, UK
UKHW041753221224
452593UK00001B/1

9 781789 635027